THE BODY
in
NARRATIVE

ISBN (paperback): 979-8-9853434-8-9
ISBN (e-book): 979-8-9853434-6-5

THE BODY *in* NARRATIVE

A Writer's Guide to Character Reactions

Action Beats | Dialogue Tags | Points of View

Franklyn James

Dedication

To the dreamers, the storytellers, writers, and lovers of verses, who dare to breathe life into words, this book is for you. To those who find solace in a solitary thought and power in the stroke of a pen or keypad, who face the daunting white canvas with courage and weave narratives that echo across time, this is for you.

To the teachers who cultivate the garden of curiosity, the readers whose minds are an ever-open theatre, and the literary explorers who believe in the transformative power of storytelling, this book is your compass.

May this guide serve as a pharos when the process seems obscure, a companion in your creative journey, and a testament to the infinite power vested in our body and emotions. Here's to your imagination's flight – may it soar!

Contents

Introduction

From Whose Point of View

I nside the bustling 3-S Café, a bubbly group sits around a table, their drinks momentarily forgotten in the wake of a lively discussion.

Pouring a fresh cup of coffee behind the counter, Alex stirs the conversation. "Ever heard of points of view in writing?"

A mischievous smile lights up Rylan's face. He leans back in his chair, eyes twinkling with mirth. "You mean like when I say, *'I danced at the club last night,'* and all that?"

Alex nods as laughter bubbles from his throat and approval flickers in his eyes. "Exactly, Rylan. That's the first-person point of view. It's intimate, personal."

Adjusting her glasses, Mrs. O'Problem joins in. Her voice is firm, yet loving. "Ah, so it's like when I tell you, *'You need to stop dancing and start praying more, Rylan.'*"

The café echoes with Alex's hearty laugh. "That's the second-person point of view, Mrs. O'Problem. It's less common but can be used effectively."

Casually resting his chin on his hands, Rylan looks playfully at Fifi. "But what if I'm talking about Fifi's latest creation? You know, saying something like, *'Fifi just knitted the most gorgeous scarf.'*"

Blushing, Fifi smiles. "Oh, that's very kind of you, dear."

A guest's voice rises above the hum of the café. "That's third-person limited. It's similar to you peeking into Fifi's world."

Mrs. O'Problem folds her hands, her gaze surveying them as she tells a story so well it's as if they're right there. *"The barista moves with practiced ease behind the counter, mind occupied with the day's chores. A handsome youth captivated by his reflection on a shiny tabletop, thoughts wandering. A woman knitting, a smile dancing on her lips as she dreams of her next project."*

As her voice fades, Fifi claps her hands, her smile widening. "Mrs. O'Problem, you've got it! That's a fine demonstration of a third-person omniscient point of view. It's like viewing the scene from above, knowing everything about everyone."

Rylan clears his throat, preparing his own tale. *"We're in the café, the heart of all the action. There's the barista, moving effortlessly behind the counter, the smooth glide of the coffee pot, the rich aroma of freshly brewed coffee filling the air. And there, tucked away in the corner, is a guy. He catches sight of someone passing by, and a slow smile spreads across his face, lighting up his eyes."*

Alex nods, understanding dawning in his eyes. "You're observing actions without assuming what anyone is thinking or feeling. That's a third-person objective or 'camera eye' perspective. Nicely done, Rylan!"

Point of View or Perspective

"...is the perspective from which the reader experience the action of story."

Rasley, A. (2008). The Power of Point of View: Make Your Story Come to Life. (pp. 9-16).

Mrs. Adina Hytte-Tikkles' voice rises softly. *"I see a barista pouring coffee, his mind already spinning with plans for the day. Meanwhile, a young man gazes out a window, lost in his world of thoughts. And there's a woman, her needles clicking together rhythmically as peace washes over her with each stitch."*

Eyes twinkling Alex comments. "Brilliantly done, Mrs. Hytte-Tikkles! That's a great example of a third-person multiple point of view. It helps build a full, rich picture of the scene."

Rylan's voice takes on a dreamy quality. *"Rylan is sitting at the café, but he's not really there. His eyes are fixed on the scene outside the window, but his mind... his mind's on a moonlit beach. The soft whisper of the waves, the cool sand under his feet, the faint taste of salt in the air."*

"Ha, ha!" laughs Mrs. O'Problem, giving Rylan a playful nudge. "You've got it. That's deep third person, and it gets really intimate. If we dive into your mind, Rylan, we'd be frolicking all day long!"

Her hands smoothing over a soft woolen scarf-in-progress, Fifi's eyes light up as she recalls, *"Remember that time we all decided to drive down to the coast together? Alex was focused on the road, his mind checking off his to-do list for the day. Rylan, in the passenger seat, his attention snagged by a billboard advertising the latest blockbuster, was already considering whether to buy tickets."*

"But that's just the surface!" Mrs. Adina Hytte-Tikkles' remarks. "We might have been passengers in the same car, but we weren't in their minds. We didn't know their deepest thoughts or their private feelings."

Alex nods, his gaze meeting each of theirs. "Yes, the contemporary omniscient. It's a toned-down version of the all-knowing perspective."

Mrs. O'Problem's voice echoes around the table, her tone wistful. *"And what if... just suppose, when your mind is in a frenzy, cascading like a relentless waterfall, with thoughts piling up, tripping over each other in a hectic dance... like whispered prayers fluttering like butterfly wings in the silence of the church..."*

Rylan raises an eyebrow, a smirk tugging at his lips. "Mrs. O'Problem, that's quite a ride you took us on! Sounds like the 'stream of consciousness' point of view to me!"

As laughter bubbles up, they all reach for their drinks, their spirits lifted by their shared discovery of the many lenses through which stories can be told.

From My Point of View

As a poet, preacher, and storyteller for over two decades, I've recently undertaken the task of transforming my devotional book into a novel. This process, while challenging, has been an exhilarating dive into the craft of writing, where I've explored various techniques and styles.

In my exploration, four key storytelling techniques have particularly stood out. These are:

- show, don't tell
- point of view (POV)

- dialogue tags
- action beats

Many writers and educators have vouched for the efficacy of these techniques in crafting compelling narratives and lifelike characters.

"Show, don't tell" is a principle that encourages writers to depict events and character emotions through detailed actions and descriptions rather than simply stating them. This approach promotes reader engagement by prompting inference and emotional investment in the story's unfolding.

"Deep point of view" refers to a narrative technique wherein the author delves deeply into a character's thoughts, feelings, and sensory experiences. The aim is to forge a closer bond between the reader and the character by letting the reader perceive the world through the character's perspective, fostering a heightened sense of empathy and connection.

Deep point of view (POV) can be used in various combinations of person (first, second, and third) and tense (present, past, and future) allowing the writer to immerse the reader in the character's perspective and create a more intimate reading experience. Below are illustrations of how deep POV can be applied across different perspectives and tenses.

First Person Deep POV: In first-person deep POV, the story is narrated from the perspective of the protagonist or a character using the pronoun "I." The narrative immerses the reader directly into the character's thoughts, emotions, and experiences.

For example:

- Present Tense: "I walk into the room, my heart pounding with anticipation."
- Past Tense: "I walked into the room, my heart pounding with anticipation."
- Future Tense: "I will walk into the room, my heart pounding with anticipation."

Second Person Deep POV: Second person deep POV addresses the reader directly using the pronoun "you," creating a sense of immediacy and involvement. This perspective is less commonly used in fiction, but it can be a powerful way to engage the reader.

For example:

- Present Tense: "You enter the room, your heart pounding with anticipation."
- Past Tense: "You entered the room, your heart pounding with anticipation."
- Future Tense: "You will enter the room, your heart pounding with anticipation."

Third Person Deep POV: Third-person deep POV involves using the pronouns "he," "she," or "they" to refer to the character. The narrative delves deeply into the character's thoughts, emotions, and experiences, creating a close connection between the reader and the character.

For example:

- Present Tense: "He enters the room, his heart pounding with anticipation."
- Past Tense: "He entered the room, his heart pounding with anticipation."
- Future Tense: "He will enter the room, his heart pounding with anticipation."

Illustration of "Show, Don't Tell" and "Deep POV"

Tell

The vervet monkey is naturally curious but easily frightened by sudden movements.

Show

Suspended in the high branches, the vervet monkey watched the humans with an air of inquisitive fascination. Its amber eyes flicked from face to face, tiny fingers curling and uncurling around the bark in anticipation. The rustle of a lunch box opening was a siren call, drawing it closer, boldened by the allure of a potential meal. But then, a child below shrieked in delight, his arms flailing wildly. The sudden movement hit the monkey like a thunderclap. With a startled yelp, it recoiled, bounding further into the leafy veil, its heart pounding like a drum against its ribcage.

In the "show" version, we demonstrate the vervet monkey's curiosity and its apprehension toward sudden movements through its actions, reactions, and emotions, instead of stating them explicitly. Readers are pulled into the monkey's perspective, and deeply engrossed in its experiences.

However, when the narrative perspective shifts abruptly – let's say, to the child who shrieked – it can create a jarring effect for the readers, akin to how the monkey is startled by the child's sudden movement.

Tag Lines or Dialogue Tags

"A tag line is a couple of words or a phrase that tells you who is speaking. The simplest and least obtrusive tag lines are 'he said' and 'she said.'"

Turco, L., & Foyie, F. (1989). Dialogue: A Socratic Dialogue on the Art of Writing Dialogue in Fiction (p. 15).

This sudden pivot can yank readers out of the immersive environment that had been meticulously built, causing a disorienting break in their engagement with the narrative.

This serves as a reminder that in our writing, we must handle shifts in point of view with care. Similar to our primate friend's reaction to unexpected change, readers too may react unfavorably to abrupt shifts in narrative perspective, disrupting their immersion and potentially diminishing the impact of our storytelling.

Shallow Point of View [Shallow POV]

Shallow point of view refers to a narrative style that maintains a certain distance between the reader and the character's thoughts and emotions. It provides an objective and detached perspective, focusing on external actions rather than the character's internal experiences. In shallow point of view, the narrator recounts events without delving deeply into the character's inner world.

This narrative style employs an observational approach, emphasizing external details over internal reflections. Let's identify these with brief explanations and examples of shallow point of view in different perspectives and tenses:

First Person Shallow POV: In first-person shallow POV, the narrator recounts events from their perspective but doesn't delve deeply into their thoughts and emotions. The narrative tends to focus more on external actions and observations.

For example:

- Present Tense: "I walk into the room, feeling a sense of anticipation."
- Past Tense: "I walked into the room, feeling a sense of anticipation."
- Future Tense: "I will walk into the room, feeling a sense of anticipation."

Second Person Shallow POV: Second-person shallow POV addresses the reader directly but maintains a more objective tone, focusing on actions and observations rather than internal experiences.

For example:

- Present Tense: "You enter the room, sensing an atmosphere of anticipation."
- Past Tense: "You entered the room, sensing an atmosphere of anticipation."
- Future Tense: "You will enter the room, sensing an atmosphere of anticipation."

Third Person Shallow POV: In third-person shallow POV, the narrator remains at a distance from the characters, providing an objective account of events and actions without delving deeply into their thoughts and emotions.

For example:

- Present Tense: "He enters the room, noticing the palpable sense of anticipation."
- Past Tense: "He entered the room, noticing the palpable sense of anticipation."
- Future Tense: "He will enter the room, noticing the palpable sense of anticipation."

The main goal of *The The Body in Narrative: A Writer's Guide to Character Reactions* isn't to delve comprehensively into the principles of "show, don't tell" and "deep point of view," but rather to provide you with a basic understanding of these concepts, so you can

Beats or Action Beats

"... are the bits of action interspersed through a scene, such as a character walking to a window or removing his glasses and rubbing his eyes—the literary equivalent of what is known in the theater as 'stage business.'"

Browne, R., & King, D. (2004). Self-Editing for Fiction Writers (2nd ed., p. 143)

engage effectively with the materials presented here. For a more in-depth exploration of these principles, there is an extensive library of resources available on these topics that you can consult at your convenience. Additionally, this guide will focus on the usage of "dialogue tags" and "action beats" and how to effectively use different body parts in your writing, even though we will be employing the "deep point of view" and "show, don't tell" style of writing.

"Dialogue tags" are phrases that identify the speaker in a conversation, typically utilizing verbs such as "said," "asked," "replied," and so forth. But they do more than just attributing dialogue to characters. They can also depict the manner of speech or describe the speaker's actions, providing the reader with added context and clarity.

"Action beats" are instances in the narrative where actions are used to break up, emphasize, or punctuate dialogue, creating a rhythm that mirrors the natural ebb and flow of conversation and thought. Although the term "action beats" is not commonly found in formal literary resources, it is widely recognized and used within the realm of authors and writing communities to define these specific narrative movements.

They involve physical actions or movements performed by characters within a scene, enhancing pacing, providing visual cues, and creating a dynamic and engaging reading experience for the audience.

Illustration using dialogue tags, body parts, and action beats

Sage stepped off the bus, shivering in anticipation. "Something's wrong," she thought, nervously scanning the quiet street. Her heart pounded in her chest as she walked toward her apartment building, her hand reaching instinctively for the can of pepper spray in her pocket.

She entered the lobby and heard a faint scratching sound coming from the elevator. *"Is it a rat scurrying across the floor?"* she wondered.

"Hello?" she called out, her voice shaking. "Is anyone there?"

Definition of Dialogue

"… While you're doing that, can I ask you a question? Sure. Go ahead.

Okay-what's dialogue?

Dialogue is a conversation.

Like what we're having right now?

Exactly.

If you already knew, why did you ask me?"

Turco, L., & Foyie, F. (1989). *Dialogue* (p. 4).

Silence greeted her. She hesitated, unsure whether to continue upstairs. Finally, she took a deep breath and stepped into the elevator, her hand hovering over the emergency button.

"Please work," she muttered under her breath, as her fingers pressed on the button.

The elevator lurched to life, and she felt her stomach drop as it began to ascend. She closed her eyes, willing herself to stay calm. When the doors finally opened on her floor, she let out a gasp of shock.

Standing before her was a man she had never seen before, his face twisted in a grotesque grin. He took a step toward her, and she instinctively clutched the pepper spray in her pocket.

"Who are you?" she demanded, her voice barely above a whisper.

"I'm here for you," the man replied, his eyes darting toward her pocket. "And I think it's time we had a little talk."

In the provided excerpt, various techniques like dialogue tags, usage of body parts to portray emotion, and action beats come into play, making the story more engaging and immersive.

Dialogue Tags

- "Hello?" she called out.
- "Please work," she muttered under her breath.
- "Who are you?" she demanded.
- "I'm here for you," the man replied.

Body Parts

- Her heart pounded in her chest.

- …her hand reaching instinctively for the can of pepper spray in her pocket.
- She instinctively clutched the pepper spray in her pocket.

Action Beats

- Sage stepped off the bus, shivering in anticipation.
- She entered the lobby and heard a faint scratching sound coming from the elevator.
- She took a deep breath and stepped into the elevator, her hand hovering over the emergency button.
- The elevator lurched to life, and she felt her stomach drop as it began to ascend.
- Standing before her was a man she had never seen before, his face twisted in a grotesque grin.

At the end of each section in *The Body in Narrative*, there are four tasks to complete. You can do some or all of them, as they are repetitive. Additionally, a comprehensive exercise at the end of the book allows you to apply what you have learned in a broader context of creative writing.

Turn the pages and see how using "body parts" can improve your storytelling. You'll find practical examples that can help you use these techniques in your own writing. Putting together this guide has helped me understand these ideas better and grow as a writer. Let's start this journey together and learn how to tell better stories.

Adam's apple

This is a noticeable protrusion on the front of the neck, typically more pronounced in males. It becomes more prominent during puberty and plays a role in deepening the voice.

Points of View

1. His Adam's apple bobbed with each rapid swallow, a pulsating beacon of his underlying anxiety.
2. The rhythmic ascent and descent of his Adam's apple mesmerized me as he spoke.
3. She couldn't tear her gaze away from the subtle quiver in his Adam's apple, an unspoken sign of his restrained emotions.
4. At each swallow, his bobbing Adam's apple screamed his discomfort.
5. His Adam's apple bounced in sync with his rapid drink chugging, sparking my suppressed laughter.
6. A shiver ran down my spine as her fingers traced the curve of my Adam's apple.
7. Leaning forward, his Adam's apple became the centerpiece of my vision.
8. Her gaze followed the bobbing of his Adam's apple as he enjoyed his meal.
9. A sympathetic lump rose in my throat, matching the dance of his Adam's apple with every swallow.
10. The irregular bobbing of her usually unnoticed Adam's apple betrayed her anxiety, dancing in rhythm with her wavering voice.
11. His protruding Adam's apple served as a powerful signifier of his masculinity.
12. My gaze fell on the small scar just above his Adam's apple, and a surge of curiosity clawed at me, prodding me to uncover its past.

Adrenal Glands

These glands atop the kidneys produce vital hormones such as adrenaline and cortisol. These hormones help regulate metabolism, the immune response, blood pressure, and stress responses.

Points of View

1. A surge of readiness washed over me; my adrenal glands were preparing for the imminent fight.
2. The stress had my adrenal glands spewing cortisol, exhaustion seeping into my bones.
3. A pang of fear coursed through me, my adrenal glands alerting me of the impending trouble.
4. Engrossed in the task, the hormonal rush from my adrenal glands registered as a mere blip.
5. Adrenal glands fired up, and a wave of energy prepped me for action.
6. The gunshot's echo had adrenaline flooding my system, my adrenal glands responding instantaneously.
7. Rollercoaster excitement ignited my adrenal glands, leaving an exhilarating rush.
8. Fighting to stay conscious, my adrenal glands pushed into overdrive.
9. Thoughts of the looming presentation sent my adrenal glands spiraling into a frenzy of nervous energy.
10. The passing danger had my adrenal glands easing off, ushering in a calming relief.
11. The long-term consequences of my overactive adrenal glands troubled the doctor.
12. Her adrenal glands kicked into overdrive, igniting a surge of primal focus that narrowed the world to a pinpoint.

Alveoli

Tiny air sacs within the lungs. They allow oxygen to move from the air into the bloodstream and carbon dioxide to be expelled from the blood back into the air.

Points of View

1. Drawing a deep breath, the feeling of alveoli expanding with fresh air filled him.
2. City air pollution had inflamed her alveoli, complicating her breathing.
3. Alveoli strained to keep up as breathlessness overcame me.
4. Concern etched on the doctor's face reflected years of smoking damage to her alveoli.
5. His alveoli labored for oxygen, triggering a sharp chest pain.
6. Cold air caused her alveoli to constrict, igniting a burn in her lungs.
7. Taking shallow breaths was a must; my damaged alveoli couldn't manage a heavy air intake.
8. The scuba diver sensed the pressure shift in his alveoli as he descended deeper.
9. The weakness of her alveoli forced her to keep an oxygen tank at hand, always.
10. A deep breath rushed air into his alveoli, invigorating his body.
11. Chemotherapy had wreaked havoc on her alveoli, causing persistent shortness of breath.
12. My alveoli battled to evict the foreign particles I'd inhaled, triggering an uncontrollable cough.

Ankles

The joints that connect the foot to the leg. These joints are formed by the interconnection of the tibia, fibula, and talus bones, allowing for a range of movements essential for walking, running, and standing.

Points of View

1. Twisting my ankle sent a needlelike pain shooting up my leg as ligaments stretched beyond their limit.
2. Examining my swollen ankle, a surge of frustration welled up, hinting at a looming difficulty in movement.
3. A wave of self-consciousness washed over me as my slender ankles peeped out beneath my dress.
4. My stride had to constantly adjust due to my weak ankles, treading with care to dodge any uneven terrain.
5. Navigating the uneven terrain required utmost focus to maintain ankle stability, avoiding any missteps.
6. Bearing the heavy load, I felt my ankle ligaments creaking in protest, unlike Alex's unwavering step.
7. Alex limbered up his ankles, bracing for the long walk that lay ahead.
8. The dancer's ankles, strong and nimble like Alex's, allowed graceful execution of intricate steps.
9. Forcing myself to stand up, my ankles cracked audibly, unnoticed by Alex.
10. A severe sprain sent Alex off the field, carried on a stretcher.
11. The biting cold gnawed at my exposed ankles, making me regret my choice of thin socks, while Alex seemed unfazed.
12. The sight of Alex's sturdy ankles sent an unexpected flutter through my heart.

Anus

The opening at the end of the digestive tract where the body expels waste. It plays a crucial role in the elimination process, effectively closing off the digestive system.

Points of View

1. An urgent call of nature tightened my anus, as it battled against the unexpected rush.
2. Pressure built up in my anus, signaling an imminent need for a bathroom break.
3. Persistent discomfort around my anus raised concerns, suggesting a need for additional medical tests.
4. The sight of his underwear, outlining his anus, pulled a suppressed giggle out of me.
5. I imagined an invasive procedure targeting my anus and I shivered.
6. A sudden wave of pleasure triggered an involuntary contraction of my anus.
7. Feeling vulnerable and embarrassed during the nurse's examination of my anus, I could hardly breathe.
8. A comedian's off-color joke about anuses made it a real challenge to keep a straight face.
9. Heat raced up my neck during the doctor's probing examination of my anus.
10. A gnawing pain gripped her anus, relentless and severe, forcing her to her to take a much-needed break from work for recovery.
11. A sharp, sudden pain shot through his anus, alerting him that something was not right.
12. During the yoga session, the stretch inadvertently put pressure on my anus, a sensation unfamiliar and strange.

Arch of the Foot

The curved part of the sole that spans between the ball and the heel. This feature is critical in supporting the body's weight and absorbing shock during movement, aiding balance and walking efficiency.

Points of View

1. By day's end, her arches throbbed with a dull, persistent ache.
2. His arches bulged with each step, marking the telltale sign of flat feet.
3. The insoles gave her aching arches much-needed support, easing her discomfort.
4. The podiatrist advocated orthotic shoes to remedy the flawed arch of his feet.
5. With her high arches, finding a good shoe fit was always an ordeal.
6. Stretching the arch of my foot released the built-up tension.
7. The ballerina's arches, the epitome of grace and strength, let her dance with an effortless charm.
8. Post-run, he massaged his left foot arch, soothing the tender muscles.
9. Her flip-flops slapped rhythmically against the arches of her feet as she paced.
10. Under his body weight, the arch of his foot gave way, making him stumble.
11. A sharp object piercing her foot sent a jolt of pain up her arch.
12. An old injury necessitated a brace for his weakened foot arch, lending support.

Arms

The upper limbs of the body that extend from the shoulder to the hand. They facilitate various activities such as lifting, carrying, and manipulating objects, enhancing complex movements and dexterity.

Points of View

1. His arms bulged with hard-earned muscles, the result of grueling gym sessions.
2. Each lift of the hefty weight sent twinges of pain up my arms, straining muscles unaccustomed to such exertion.
3. My tattoo, an inked echo of a painful past, etched its ghostly memories onto my arm.
4. Heaving myself up the steep incline, I relied on the strength in my arms, each pull a test of endurance.
5. My tiny fingers clung to my mother's arm, finding in her a sanctuary against the uncertainties of the world.
6. A network of scars laced my arms, each marking a survival story from life's battles.
7. I folded my arms across my chest, an unspoken challenge radiating defiance and disapproval.
8. His arms, strong and reassuring, coiled around me, offering a haven amid life's turbulence.
9. Sunlight warmed my arms, the breeze wafting away my concerns, leaving a serene calm in its wake.
10. My arms danced with grace across the canvas, each stroke echoing an intimate emotion.
11. A twinge of envy stabbed my heart watching my ex wrap his arms around his new love.
12. The weight of my injured arm, bound in a sling, served as a constant reminder of my fragile post-accident state.

Arteries

The blood vessels that carry oxygen-rich blood and essential nutrients from the heart to all body parts, supporting tissue function and overall health.

Points of View

1. My heart pounded with fear as I watched the doctor's furrowed brow, a clear sign of his concern for the blockage in my arteries.
2. Stress coursed through my body, causing my temples to throb, and I felt my arteries pulse with each beat of my heart.
3. A cold dread snaked through my arteries, coiling tight around my heart. Each pulse hammered the grim news deeper, a relentless drumbeat echoing the doctor's words. My breath hitched, and I felt a foreign sensation as if my very air supply had been choked off.
4. "The surgeon's voice was calm and reassuring," I thought, squeezing the armrest. "She said bypass surgery is needed to fix the blockage in my arteries and restore blood flow," I explained to my worried spouse with a shaky voice.
5. "Doctor, are there any other ways to improve blood flow in my arteries?" I questioned hesitantly, worry furrowing my brow. Finally, I nodded slowly and said, "Alright, I'll start taking the medication for my blood pressure to keep my arteries healthy."
6. "Can you hear that whooshing sound in my arteries, doctor?" I whispered, leaning closer to the stethoscope with a hopeful expression. "It's like the rushing of water as waves surged and receded," I commented in wonder.
7. "OMG, look at all those tiny veins and arteries!" I exclaimed, tracing the intricate network on the anatomical model with my finger. "It's incredible how complex the human body is, especially the whole artery system," I murmured in awe.

8. Fear gripped me as a sharp pain ripped through my chest, and I instinctively knew that it had something to do with my arteries. I waited anxiously for answers.

9. Anxiety overwhelmed me as I lay on the operating table, my heart racing, while the surgeon worked to widen my narrow artery through angioplasty.

10. My breathing grew labored, and my heart pounded faster as I pushed my body to the limit while running, my arteries struggling to keep up with the intense physical exertion.

11. Holding my breath, I hoped with all my heart to hear the reassuring sound of healthy blood flowing through my arteries as the doctor placed the stethoscope on my chest.

12. The tightness in my chest was a constant reminder of the plaque buildup in my arteries, and I knew that I needed to make significant lifestyle changes to improve my heart health.

Practice Exercises

Instruction: Use this exercise to deepen your understanding of the lesson after reviewing each body part, such as the Adam's Apple or zygote, or after completing all the body parts in a particular letter set—A, B, or Z.

Task 1: Tagging Dialogues: Identify and list the dialogue tags used in the examples.

Task 2: Tracking Action Beats: Analyze the provided examples and identify action beats.

Task 3: Teasing Out Narrative Styles: Review the examples and distinguish between two narrative styles. Mark instances of deep POV that immerse you in a character's emotions or thoughts with a check mark (✓). Use an asterisk (*) to denote shallow POV instances, which focus primarily on surface-level actions or descriptions.

Task 4: Testing Your Skills with New Examples: Write four new phrases or short paragraphs incorporating an action beat and a dialogue tag. Use deep and shallow POV to explore different aspects of the body part discussed in this section.

Answers to Practice Exercises for Arteries

Task 1: Tagging Dialogues
- Example 4: "thought," "explained"
- Example 5: "questioned," "said"
- Example 6: "whispered," "commented"
- Example 7: "exclaimed," "murmured"

Task 2: Tracking Action Beats
- Example 1: "Heart pounded with fear, watched the doctor's furrowed brow."
- Example 2: "Stress coursed, temples to throb, arteries pulse."
- Example 3: "A cold dread snaked, coiling tight, pulse hammered, breath hitched, I felt."
- Example 4: "Squeezing the armrest."
- Example 5: "Questioned hesitantly, worry furrowing, nodded slowly."
- Example 6: "Leaning closer to the stethoscope"
- Example 7: "Tracing the intricate network"
- Example 8: "Fear gripped, sharp pain ripped, waited anxiously."
- Example 9: "Lay on the operating table, heart racing, surgeon worked."
- Example 10: "Breathing grew labored, heart pounded faster, pushed my body, running."
- Example 11: "Holding my breath."
- Example 12: "The tightness in my chest."

Task 3: Teasing Out Narrative Styles

Example	Deep POV	Shallow POV	Comment
1	✓		
2		*	
3	✓		
4		*	
5	✓		
6		*	
7		*	
8	✓		
9	✓		
10	✓		
11	✓		
12	✓	*	Open to interpretation as both deep and shallow POV.

Task 4: Testing Your Skills with New Examples

1. My legs burned with exertion, but I pushed on, willing myself to keep running. My lungs ached, and I could feel the blood shooting through my arteries, carrying much-needed oxygen to my muscles. "Just a little further," I muttered through gritted teeth. *(Deep POV)*

2. "This is harder than I thought," I confessed, feeling the strain in my arteries as I attempted to calm my racing heart with deep breaths. *(Deep POV)*

3. "You'll need to stay still," the technician instructed, focusing intently on the ultrasound screen displaying the flow through my arteries. *(Shallow POV)*

4. "It's just a quick check," the nurse reassured me as she adjusted the cuff, her eyes scanning the monitor for my arterial pressure. *(Shallow POV)*

Note: As you may have observed from this exercise, identifying deep and shallow POV can be a nuanced process. Each reader and writer brings their unique perspective, shaped by personal experiences and artistic sensibilities. Therefore, your responses to the following exercise might be different from mine, and that's perfectly okay! This subjectivity enriches literary analysis, fostering a wide range of insights and discussions.

Back

The area of the body that extends from the shoulders to the hips. It encompasses the spine, providing structural support and flexibility. Back muscles play an essential role in movement and maintaining posture.

Points of View

1. "I strained my back lifting that heavy box," I grunted through gritted teeth.
2. He winced in pain as he rubbed his sore back, muttering to himself, "Should've been more careful with that heavy box."
3. Twisting my back, I craned my neck to get a better view of the painting on the wall, thinking to myself how lovely it looked.
4. "Just relax," the chiropractor said as he adjusted my back, his hands working to relieve the tension in my muscles.
5. Closing my eyes, I felt the warmth of the sun on my back and let out a contented sigh, "This is perfect."
6. "That dragon tattoo on your back looks incredible," I commented, admiring the shimmering scales in the light.
7. Struggling to keep up with the weight of the backpack on my back, I groaned, "This is heavier than I thought it would be."
8. "Sleeping on my back after the surgery was uncomfortable, but it was necessary for my recovery," I explained to my friend.
9. Rylan threw his head back, let out a booming laugh that echoed off the walls. "That was hilarious!" he bellowed.
10. Leaning, my back against the chair, I closed my eyes and took a deep breath, trying to calm my racing thoughts.
11. "I have a scar on my back from a childhood accident," she confided, trying to hide the pain in her voice.
12. "I felt a chill run down my back as the ghostly figure appeared before me, its icy breath sending shivers through my body," said Brea.

Bile ducts

Tubes that transport bile from the liver to the small intestine. Bile is crucial for digestion, particularly in breaking down fats, making these ducts essential for efficient nutrient absorption.

Points of View

1. The putrid stench clawed at my throat, triggering a violent gag reflex. "It's like bile's trying to force its way up my ducts!" I sputtered, my stomach churning in revolt.
2. My concern bled into my voice as I asked the doctor, "Could a blockage in my bile ducts lead to liver damage?"
3. A sharp pain lanced my side, causing me to voice her fear, "Could this be a problem with my bile ducts?"
4. Groggy from anesthesia, she asked the surgeon, "Was it my bile ducts causing the severe abdominal pain?"
5. Studying the anatomy chart, I pointed out to my study partner, "Look how the bile ducts twist and turn from the liver into the intestines."
6. The doctor's voice was somber. "A tumor is blocking the bile ducts. We'll need to perform surgery to remove it."
7. Anxiety seeped into my voice as I asked the surgeon, "Do I need a cholecystectomy? Will it help protect my bile ducts by removing the gallbladder?"
8. Relief washed over her as she told her husband, "The test results show my bile ducts are working just fine. I'm so relieved."
9. He furrowed his brows, a dull ache throbbing in the pit of his stomach. "Do I need this medication to regulate the flow through my bile ducts?" he pressed the pharmacist, hoping it would chase away the sluggish feeling.

10. The idea sparked a flicker of curiosity, but a strange tightness constricted her gut. "Cooking with bile? Does that involve the bile ducts somehow?" she queried her culinary instructor, the thought sending a tremor through her digestive system.

11. She winced as a searing cramp twisted through her abdomen. "Doctor, could this pain be a sign of something wrong with my bile ducts?" she inquired, a knot of worry tightening around them.

12. He grimaced, the greasy food sitting heavy in his stomach. "Ugh, I think I overdid it. Feeling a dull pressure, almost like a blockage, around my bile ducts," he mumbled, regretting his indulgence.

Bladder

A muscular sac located in the pelvis, the bladder stores urine until it is ready to be expelled from the body. This organ expands as it fills and contracts during urination.

Points of View

1. The urge to pee threatened to overcome me, my bladder feeling as if it might explode. "Mrs. O'Problem," I gasped, "we need to find a bathroom. Now."
2. A persistent dull ache nestled in my lower abdomen had me concerned. Turning to the doctor, I asked, "Could this be a bladder problem?"
3. "Mr. O'Problem, we must insert a catheter to drain your bladder. Your enlarged prostate is causing a blockage," said the nurse.
4. "There, Mrs. O'Problem, see that round sac? That's your bladder, filled with urine."
5. A vulnerability surfaced as I confided, "Since my spinal injury, I've lost control over my bladder. I've had to resort to adult diapers."
6. "I regularly drink cranberry juice; it's my armor against the bladder infections I'm so prone to getting," I shared with a friend.
7. The sound of urine splashing in the toilet water was a chorus of relief. "Ah, the sweet release of an empty bladder," I exhaled.
8. The doctor's solemn tone made my heart drop. "I regret to inform you, Mr. O'Problem, that bladder cancer has spread to your lymph nodes. We need to start aggressive treatment immediately."

9. I woke up several times in the night, my bladder urging me out of my warm, comfortable bed. "Not again," I groaned to the darkness, frustrated by my body's refusal to let me sleep uninterrupted.

10. Desperation edged into my voice as I turned to Mrs. O'Problem in the car. "I've been trying everything to distract myself," I confessed, feeling the pressure building in my bladder. "But I don't think I can hold it much longer."

11. Emerging from the restroom, relief washed over me, warm and welcome. "Thank goodness for that," I sighed, my bladder feeling blissfully empty. "I was starting to think my bladder and I were on a never-ending quest for a bathroom."

12. In the safety of the support group, I shared my struggle. "Urinary incontinence is a constant battle," I admitted, my voice tight. "The fear of a sudden leak from my bladder keeps me isolated and, frankly, embarrassed."

Blood vessels

A network of tubes that transport blood throughout the body. They include arteries, veins, and capillaries, each playing a unique role in the circulation system.

Points of View

1. "The doctor pored over my scans, tracing the highways of blood vessels, looking for any sign of disease," I explained, my tone mirroring the worry creased on my face.
2. "Excitement pulsed through my veins with every beat of my heart. I could almost see a riot of sensations coursing through my blood vessels," Fifi replied, eyes sparkling with anticipation.
3. "Ah!" Fifi winced, her face scrunching as the needle pierced her skin. "It's as if it went straight into my blood vessels."
4. "Look, Fifi, see that?" I pointed to the X-ray, a stark black-and-white map of our insides. "A veritable forest of blood vessels branching out in every direction."
5. "I've heard of this genetic disorder," Fifi said thoughtfully. "It weakens the blood vessels and triggers sudden, torrential nosebleeds."
6. "To combat my high blood pressure, Fifi, I pop these little pills. They relax my blood vessels and ease the rush of blood through my body," I explained, rolling a tiny tablet in my palm.
7. "Oh, the embarrassment!" Fifi flushed, covering her face with her hands. "I felt my blood vessels expand as my cheeks burned hot with a blush."
8. "Poor man," I sighed, sympathizing with Fifi's uncle. "His legs, always aching and swollen because of those gnarled, inefficient blood vessels."

9. "Every day, I thank the health of my blood vessels," Fifi said, a note of genuine gratitude in her voice. They let me live this active, vibrant life."

10. "Did you know," Fifi started, her eyes gleaming with newfound knowledge, "that regular jogging can strengthen our blood vessels?"

11. "They cut me open, you know," Fifi shared, her voice barely a whisper. "Had to repair a weakened blood vessel in my heart that was causing the relentless chest pain."

12. "His brain..." The words caught in my throat, choked by a sudden surge of terror. A blood vessel had burst in his head, sending a horrifying realization crashing over me. The image of our friend struggling to move his limbs flashed through my mind, each desperate twitch starkly contrasting with his usually fluid movements.

Bone marrow

The soft tissue inside bones that acts as a factory for blood cells. It produces red blood cells, which carry oxygen; white blood cells, which fight infections; and platelets, which help blood clot.

Points of View

1. "Shaquille, the doctor's going to sample your bone marrow. He wants to rule out leukemia," I explained, my eyes trained on his for any sign of apprehension.
2. "You wouldn't believe it, Shaquille. I watched a nurse today giving a bone marrow transplant. It was for a patient with a rare blood disorder," I shared, still in awe.
3. "There it was, under the microscope," Shaquille marveled. "Bone marrow, a universe of cells in a drop of vibrant red."
4. "Shaquille, I'm sorry," I sighed. "You'll need to take drugs to stimulate your bone marrow. The chemotherapy took its toll."
5. "You did something incredible, Shaquille," I said with admiration. "Your sister needed a bone marrow transplant, and you stepped up."
6. "Shaquille, I hate to tell you this, but your bone marrow cancer's spread," I said, my voice catching on the words. "We'll need to start an aggressive treatment protocol."
7. "You've got a tough road ahead, John. Your genetic disorder causes the bone marrow to churn out faulty blood cells. It's causing your anemia," I said, hoping my empathy came through.
8. "Don't fret, Shaquille. We'll take a bone marrow sample to figure out why you're losing weight so fast," I reassured him, trying to alleviate his concern.
9. "I am incredibly proud of you, Shaquille. You saved a life with your bone marrow donation," I said, my voice filled with admiration.

10. "Would you like more tea, dear?" Fifi asked, her gaze fixated on the report in her hands. "Leukemia... bone marrow transplant." She let the words settle in the silence of the kitchen.

11. "Never understood the hype of bone marrow. Give me the juicy meat any day," Shaquille chuckled, discarding the picked-clean bone.

12. "Maybe I should get my bone marrow checked," Shaquille quipped, his grin faltering briefly as he took a thoughtful bite of the chicken. "Never hurts to be cautious, right? Especially with all this talk of bone marrow these days."

Bones

The complex, rigid structures that make up the body's skeleton. They support the body, protect internal organs, and work with muscles to allow movement. Bones also store minerals and help produce blood cells.

Points of View

1. "The doctor ordered an X-ray to check for fractures in my bones after the car accident," I thought.
2. "I feel a sharp pain in my bones," she said. "It could indicate a problem with my joints or osteoporosis."
3. "We need to insert metal rods to stabilize the broken bones in your leg," the surgeon explained.
4. "Look at the bones on the anatomy chart," I pointed out. "They are a complex network of joints and connections."
5. "I have to wear a cast to immobilize the bones in my arm," he said. "They were fractured in a fall."
6. "I take calcium supplements to strengthen my bones and prevent osteoporosis," she shared.
7. "I could feel my bones creaking as I stretched my arms after a long day at the computer," I observed.
8. "The bone cancer has spread to my ribs," he said. "It's causing me excruciating pain and difficulty breathing."
9. "I suffer from a rare genetic disorder," she explained. "It causes my bones to be abnormally shaped and brittle, leading to frequent fractures."
10. "I had to have surgery to remove a tumor that was pressing against my spinal bones," I shared. "It was causing paralysis."
11. "I feel a sense of wonder at the complexity and strength of the human skeletal system," she said, "marveling at how the bones can support the body's weight and withstand impact."
12. "We have to do a bone density scan to check for signs of osteoporosis," the doctor informed me.

Bottom

The lower part of the torso, including the buttocks and anus. This area plays a role in sitting, supporting internal organs, and the excretion process.

Points of View

1. "The doctor examined my bottom to check for signs of hemorrhoids," I winced in discomfort.
2. "I feel a twinge in my bottom," she said, "which could indicate a muscle strain or nerve damage."
3. "Let's change the dressings on the surgical incision near your bottom," the nurse suggested to the patient.
4. "Look at the stretch marks on my bottom," she lamented. "They're evidence of weight gain and loss over the years."
5. "I have to sit on a donut-shaped cushion," he said, "to relieve pressure on my bottom, which is sore from prolonged sitting."
6. "I'll apply cream to soothe the diaper rash on my infant's bottom," she said, "to make her more comfortable."
7. "I could feel the cool breeze on my bottom," I laughed, "as I skinny-dipped in the lake."
8. "The bottom surgery has transformed my body," he said, "giving me a new sense of confidence and identity."
9. "My chronic constipation causes pain and discomfort in my bottom," he explained to his doctor.
10. "I had to have a colonoscopy," I shared, "to screen for colon cancer, which required inserting a tube through my bottom."
11. "Finally, I found a comfortable position for my bottom," she sighed with relief, "after the long flight."
12. "Let's do a pelvic exam to check for any issues," the gynecologist said to her patient, "including the bottom."

Brain

The central organ of the nervous system, housed within the skull. It controls the body's functions, governing thoughts, emotions, and physical movements. This complex organ also handles memory, senses, and decision-making, determining how we interact with our environments.

Points of View

1. The doctor ordered an MRI to check for abnormalities in my brain after I had a seizure.
2. She felt a sense of clarity in her brain after a good night's sleep, ready to tackle the day ahead.
3. The neurosurgeon performed a delicate operation on the tumor in his brain, using advanced technology to minimize the risk of damage.
4. I could see the different parts of the brain on the 3D model, each responsible for a specific function.
5. He had to take medication to manage his anxiety, which helped to calm his overactive brain.
6. She practiced mindfulness meditation to quiet the chatter in her brain and reduce stress.
7. I could feel my brain buzzing with excitement as I prepared to give the presentation.
8. The brain injury had left him with cognitive deficits, struggling to remember basic information and perform simple tasks.
9. He suffered from a genetic disorder that caused progressive degeneration of the brain, leading to dementia.
10. I had to have a brain biopsy to diagnose the cause of my unexplained headaches and fatigue.
11. She felt a sense of awe at the complexity and power of the human brain, amazed by its ability to learn and adapt.
12. "I can't believe how much information my brain can process in a single moment," she marveled.

Breastbone

The flat bone located in the center of the chest, known as the sternum. It serves as the primary connection point for the ribs, helping to protect vital organs like the heart and lungs within the thoracic cavity.

Points of View

1. "The doctor palpated my breastbone to check for tenderness or swelling."
2. She felt a sharp pain in her breastbone, which could indicate a fractured rib or a heart attack.
3. The surgeon made an incision in the breastbone to access his heart for the bypass surgery.
4. "I could see the breastbone on the X-ray – a long narrow bone with a distinctive shape."
5. "He had to wear a brace to immobilize the breastbone after the car accident, which had caused multiple fractures."
6. "She took pain medication to manage the discomfort in her breastbone after the chest surgery."
7. "I could feel my breastbone vibrating with the beat of the music at the concert."
8. "The breastbone cancer had spread to other parts of the body, requiring aggressive chemotherapy and radiation."
9. "He suffered from a rare congenital disorder that caused his breastbone to protrude outward, making it difficult to breathe."
10. "I had to have a CT scan to check for any abnormalities in my breastbone, which had been causing persistent pain."
11. "She felt a sense of relief after the doctor reassured her that the lump in her breastbone was benign."
12. "I winced as the doctor pressed down on my breastbone, checking for any signs of tenderness," the patient said.

Bronchi

The bronchi consist of two tubes, the left, and the right, which branch from the trachea and lead directly into each lung. They are essential passageways for air moving in and out of the lungs and facilitate breathing.

Points of View

1. "The doctor listened to my lungs and heard wheezing in the bronchi, indicating asthma."
2. "She felt a tightness in her chest, a sign of inflammation in the bronchi due to a respiratory infection."
3. "The respiratory therapist taught him how to do deep breathing exercises to clear the mucus from his bronchi."
4. "I could see the bronchi on the CT scan, narrow tubes that branched out like a tree."
5. "He had to use a nebulizer to deliver medication directly to his bronchi, which helped to open up the airways."
6. "She coughed up phlegm from her bronchi, a common symptom of bronchitis."
7. "I could feel the vibration in my chest as I coughed, trying to clear the congestion in my bronchi."
8. "The bronchiectasis had caused permanent damage to his bronchi, making it difficult for him to breathe."
9. "He suffered from chronic obstructive pulmonary disease (COPD), a progressive condition that affects the bronchi and lungs."
10. "I have to have a bronchoscopy to check for any abnormalities in my bronchi, which will require inserting a tube through my nose or mouth."
11. "She felt a sense of gratitude for the doctors and nurses who had helped her recover from the severe pneumonia that had affected her bronchi."
12. "As I took a deep breath, I felt the air travel down my bronchi and into my lungs, grateful for the ability to breathe freely."

Bronchioles

Small tubes that branch off from the larger airways in the lungs called bronchi. They lead to tiny air sacs known as alveoli, where the body takes in oxygen and releases carbon dioxide.

Points of View

1. "The doctor explained that the inflammation in her bronchioles was causing the shortness of breath and wheezing."
2. "She felt a constriction in her chest, a sign that her bronchioles were constricted due to an allergic reaction."
3. "The respiratory therapist taught him how to use a peak flow meter to monitor the function of his bronchioles."
4. "I could see the bronchioles on the lung function test, tiny tubes that looked like a network of branches."
5. "He had to use a bronchodilator to relax the muscles in his bronchioles, which helped to improve his breathing."
6. "She felt a tickle in her throat, a sign that her bronchioles were irritated due to exposure to smoke or pollution."
7. "I could feel the air flowing through my bronchioles as I took a deep breath in."
8. "The bronchiolitis had caused severe inflammation in his bronchioles, requiring hospitalization and intensive treatment."
9. "He suffered from cystic fibrosis, a genetic disorder that affects the function of the bronchioles and other organs."
10. "I had to have a bronchiole biopsy to diagnose the cause of my persistent cough and shortness of breath."
11. "She felt a sense of relief after the doctor prescribed a course of antibiotics to treat the infection in her bronchioles."
12. "The nurse demonstrated the proper technique for using an inhaler to deliver medication directly to the bronchioles."

Buttocks

The two round, fleshy parts at the lower rear of the human trunk, commonly referred to as the rear, backside, behind, bum, glutes, rump, seat, tush, or tail. This area forms the surface on which a person sits.

Points of View

1. "The doctor examined the rash on my buttocks, which could be a sign of a skin infection."
2. "She felt a sharp pain in her buttocks, a sign of a muscle strain or injury."
3. "The physical therapist taught him exercises to strengthen his buttocks muscles, which had been weakened due to prolonged sitting."
4. "I could see the dimples on her buttocks, a sign of cellulite, which is common in women."
5. "He had to use a cushion to relieve the pressure on his buttocks, which had become sore due to sitting for long periods of time."
6. "She felt embarrassed about the cellulite on her buttocks, but the personal trainer assured her that it was a normal part of the body."
7. "I could feel the tension in my buttocks muscles as I stood up from the chair, a sign of stiffness due to lack of movement."
8. "The injection in his buttocks helped to relieve the pain from the sciatic nerve, which was causing discomfort in his leg."
9. "He suffered from piriformis syndrome, a condition that causes pain and discomfort in the buttocks due to the compression of the sciatic nerve."
10. "I had to have a biopsy of a lump on my buttocks, which was found to be a lipoma, a benign fatty tumor."
11. "She felt a sense of satisfaction after completing the squats and lunges that targeted her buttocks muscles during her workout."
12. "He could see the bruise on his son's buttocks, a result of falling off his bike earlier that day."

Practice Exercises

Instruction: Use this exercise to deepen your understanding of the lesson after reviewing each body part, such as the Adam's Apple or zygote, or after completing all the body parts in a particular letter set—A, B, or Z.

Task 1: Tagging Dialogues: Identify and list the dialogue tags used in the examples.

Task 2: Tracking Action Beats: Analyze the provided examples and identify action beats.

Task 3: Teasing Out Narrative Styles: Review the examples and distinguish between two narrative styles. Mark instances of deep POV that immerse you in a character's emotions or thoughts with a check mark (✓). Use an asterisk (*) to denote shallow POV instances, which focus primarily on surface-level actions or descriptions.

Task 4: Testing Your Skills with New Examples: Write four new phrases or short paragraphs incorporating an action beat and a dialogue tag. Use deep and shallow POV to explore different aspects of the body part discussed in this section.

Capillaries

These are tiny blood vessels that connect arteries and veins and deliver oxygen and nutrients to cells and tissues throughout the body.

Points of View

1. "I can't believe this is happening," Sage thought to herself as her heart raced and the capillaries in her fingertips pulsed with excitement.
2. "Ouch!" Rylan winced as the doctor inserted the needle into a capillary in his arm, drawing blood for testing.
3. "It's amazing," Sage whispered in awe as she marveled at the intricate network of capillaries visible in the microscope slide. "Each one is a vital pathway for life."
4. "I can't take it anymore," Rylan sobbed as the capillaries in his eyes burst and tears streamed down his face, overwhelmed with emotion.
5. "Oh, no, I'm blushing," Sage thought to herself as she felt the capillaries in her cheeks flushing with embarrassment. "I hope he didn't notice."
6. "I can barely feel my fingers," Rylan said through chattering teeth as the capillaries constricted and reduced blood flow to his extremities.
7. "Yes, that's it!" Sage exclaimed, feeling a buzz of energy in the capillaries of her brain as she had a sudden burst of inspiration.
8. "I can't catch my breath," Rylan gasped as the capillaries in his lungs struggled to keep up with his rapid breathing.
9. "Ow, my nose!" Sage exclaimed as she felt a sharp pain, and the capillaries in her nose ruptured, causing a nosebleed.
10. "I can feel the burn," Rylan grunted as the capillaries in his muscles worked overtime and burned with exertion as he pushed himself to the limit.

11. "Oh no, what happened?" Sage thought to herself as her heart sank when she saw the dark purple bruises, evidence of burst capillaries beneath her skin.

12. "Come on, brain, work with me," Rylan muttered. He could sense the capillaries in his brain working overtime as he struggled to solve the complex problem.

Cheeks

These are the fleshy parts of the face situated below the eyes and extending towards the ears. They cover portions of the jawbone and are instrumental in facial expressions, such as smiling and blushing.

Points of View

1. Sage's cheeks flushed with embarrassment as she realized her mistake.
2. Rylan felt a warm sensation in his cheeks as he smiled at the kind stranger who held the door for him.
3. The cool air made Sage's cheeks numb as she walked outside in the winter weather.
4. Rylan couldn't help but grin, feeling the muscles in his cheeks stretch as he watched the funny video.
5. Sage's cheeks ached from smiling so much during the photoshoot.
6. The makeup artist gently applied blush to Rylan's cheeks, giving him a rosy glow.
7. Sage's cheeks felt hot and itchy from the sunburn she got at the beach.
8. Rylan suppressed a laugh, feeling the muscles in his cheeks twitching as he tried to keep a straight face.
9. Tears streamed down Sage's cheeks as she cried uncontrollably.
10. Rylan's cheeks hurt from clenching his jaw so tightly during the stressful meeting.
11. Sage felt a sense of pride as her cheeks puffed up with air, blowing out the candles on her birthday cake.
12. Rylan's heart skipped a beat as he saw the dimples forming on her cheeks when she smiled.

Chest

This is the upper front part of the body that houses vital organs like the heart and lungs, all protected by the ribcage. It plays a significant role in the respiratory and circulatory systems.

Points of View

1. "I can't handle this," Sage thought, her chest tightening with anxiety as she anticipated the upcoming exam.
2. "What's happening to me?" Rylan wondered, feeling a sudden pang in his chest as if his heart had skipped a beat.
3. "Take a deep breath for me," the doctor instructed, listening carefully to Rylan's chest with a stethoscope and checking for abnormalities.
4. Sage took a deep breath, feeling her chest expand.
5. "It's like the weight of the world is on my chest," Rylan admitted.
6. "This is amazing," Sage whispered, her heart racing with excitement and a fluttering sensation in her chest.
7. "I miss them so much," Rylan thought, feeling a dull ache in his chest as he remembered the loss of loved ones.
8. "I can't hold it in any longer," Sage sobbed, her chest heaving as she cried.
9. "I did it!" Rylan exclaimed with a grin, his chest swelling with pride as he received recognition for his achievements.
10. "This is so beautiful," Sage said, her chest feeling tight with emotion as she listened to the touching speech.
11. "You had no right to do that," Rylan said, his chest burning with rage as he confronted the person who had wronged him.
12. "I love you all so much," Sage said, her chest filling with warmth as she hugged her loved ones tightly.

Chin

The protruding part of the face located below the mouth and above the neck, forming the lower edge of the jaw.

Points of View

1. My teeth sank into my lip, causing a sharp pain to shoot through my chin. I cursed under my breath, annoyed at my own clumsiness.
2. I stood my ground, my chin jutting out stubbornly as I refused to back down from the argument. My heart pounded in my chest, but I wouldn't let him see my fear.
3. Lost in thought, I rested my chin in my hand. My mind raced with possibilities, but I couldn't make sense of them all.
4. I tried to hold back the tears, but my chin trembled uncontrollably. I felt exposed, vulnerable, and alone.
5. Fear gripped me, causing my chin to quiver uncontrollably. This was it – the moment I'd been dreading. I took a deep breath and stepped forward, hoping I wouldn't falter.
6. I refused to be pushed around any longer. With determination burning in my chest, I lifted my chin defiantly and met their gaze head-on.
7. His laugh echoed through the room, and I couldn't help but smile at the sight of the dimple in his chin. It was like a secret shared only between us.
8. The disappointment hit me like a ton of bricks, and my chin dropped in defeat. I'd trained so hard for this, but it wasn't enough.
9. His chin was rough against my fingertips, and I marveled at the texture of his beard. It was a small moment of intimacy, but it made my heart race.
10. I took a deep breath and lifted my chin up high. I was nervous, but I wouldn't let them see it. I had to project confidence, even if I didn't feel it.

11. I tried to brush off the pain, but my scraped and bruised chin throbbed with every movement. I refused to show weakness, even though every fiber of my being was screaming for help.

12. I rested my chin on his shoulder, feeling safe and protected in his embrace. It was a moment of vulnerability, but I trusted him completely.

Clavicle

Also known as the collarbone: These bones connect the shoulder blades to the breastbone and provide structural support to the shoulders. They also aid in arm movements.

Points of View

1. I gasped, clutching my clavicle as a sharp pain shot through me. The sound of the accident still rang in my ears, and I couldn't shake the feeling of dread.
2. He wore the sling like a badge of honor, a reminder of his bravery on the field. But the pain radiating from his broken clavicle was a constant reminder that even heroes could be hurt.
3. She couldn't help but admire the curve of her clavicle, the elegant line of bone that connected her shoulder to her neck. It was a small detail, but it made her feel beautiful.
4. Sweat gathered at my temples as I glanced at the clock. Ten minutes until the presentation, and my preparation was still inadequate. My heart pounded in my chest, each beat sending a resonating shockwave up to my clavicle.
5. The sight of his protruding clavicle made my stomach churn. I didn't want to be here, but I couldn't look away.
6. She winced as she rubbed her sore clavicle, cursing herself for sleeping in an awkward position. The day had barely started, and she was already in pain.
7. The strength of the clavicle never ceased to amaze me. It was a small bone, but it held everything together. Without it, we'd fall apart.
8. He gritted his teeth, trying to hide the pain in his bruised clavicle. He couldn't let the team down, no matter what.
9. She cradled her hand over her clavicle, trying to protect it from any further damage. It was fragile, but it was hers.

10. The doctor's words were a relief, a weight lifted off my chest. My clavicle wasn't broken, and I could finally breathe again.
11. The itching was unbearable, a constant reminder of the wound on his clavicle. He knew he shouldn't scratch it, but the temptation was too great.
12. The pain was excruciating, shooting through her clavicle like a bolt of lightning. She knew she'd strained a muscle, but she couldn't afford to rest. There was too much to do.

Collarbone

Also known as the clavicle: This bone runs horizontally across the top of the chest, between the shoulder and the neck.

Points of View

1. My collarbone ached as I tried to move my arm after the injury.
2. His collarbone was fractured, and he had to wear a brace to support his shoulder.
3. She traced the delicate curve of the collarbone with her finger, marveling at its beauty.
4. My collarbone was exposed after the accident, a gruesome sight that made me sick to my stomach.
5. His collarbone protruded from his skin like a jagged edge, evidence of the violent impact.
6. She winced as she felt a sharp pain in her collarbone, realizing she had pulled a muscle.
7. My collarbone clicked as I lifted my arm, a sign that it was still healing.
8. His collarbone was bruised and swollen, but he tried to hide it under his shirt.
9. She felt a sense of relief when the doctor confirmed that her collarbone was not broken.
10. My collarbone throbbed with pain after the surgery, but I knew it was a necessary procedure.
11. His collarbone was aching from the long hours spent hunched over the computer, a reminder to take breaks and stretch.
12. She held her breath as the doctor examined her collarbone, anxious for the diagnosis.

Colon

A long, muscular tube that forms part of the digestive system, primarily responsible for absorbing water and electrolytes from digested food. This process helps form solid waste that is expelled from the body.

Points of View

1. Rubbing his stomach, he told his co-worker, "I have to watch what I eat. My colon doesn't take kindly to certain foods and gets really irritated." *Shallow POV, action beat, and dialogue tags are used.*

2. A twinge in my gut made me anxious. My face must have shown my worry because my partner looked concerned. "Something's not right with my colon. I think I need to see a doctor." I reached for the phone, fingers trembling. *Deep POV and action beats are used.*

3. Marah doubled over, gasping. "My stomach feels like a thousand suns are burning inside." She wiped away tears that had started to form. "I haven't had anything clean to eat in days. Maybe something bad got into my colon." *Shallow POV with dialogue tag and action beats.*

4. The pain in my gut was unbearable. My colon felt twisted and unyielding. "What can I do to relieve this constipation?" I groaned to my doctor, desperation in my eyes. *Deep POV, action beat, and dialogue tags are used.*

5. His voice trembled as he admitted to his wife, "I'm scared of what they might find in my colon. What if it's cancer?" *Shallow POV, dialogue tags are used.*

6. Taking a healthy bite of her fiber-filled salad, she said to her friend, determination in her voice, "I'm doing everything to keep my colon healthy. No more processed foods for me." *Deep POV, action beat, and dialogue tags are used.*

7. Clutching his abdomen, he muttered, "I can't ignore this pain in my colon any longer. It's time to get this checked out." *Shallow POV, dialogue tags are used.*

8. Confiding in his therapist, his voice barely above a whisper, he said, "I don't know how to handle this news about my colon. I'm so afraid." *Deep POV, action beat, and dialogue tags are used.*

9. My cheeks flushed as I told the doctor, "I feel embarrassed talking about my colon, but I know it's crucial for my health." *Shallow POV and dialogue tags are used.*

10. She leaned in and whispered to her sister, concern in her eyes, "I scheduled a colonoscopy just to make sure my colon's okay." *Deep POV and dialogue tags are used.*

11. Bright-eyed and hopeful, she shared with her nutritionist, "I'm trying to find natural ways to support my colon. Do you have any suggestions?" *Shallow POV and dialogue tags are used.*

12. I raised my glass of water during dinner and announced to my family, a proud smile on my face, "I'm changing my diet to take better care of my colon. It's time to prioritize my health." *Deep POV, action beat, and dialogue tags are used.*

Note: The examples given here illustrate the use of shallow and deep points of view, action beats, and dialogue tags, as previously defined. The distinctions between action beats and dialogue tags can be subtle and sometimes overlap, leading to different interpretations by writers and readers. These nuances highlight the complexity and flexibility of narrative tools, and careful attention to them can enrich the writing process.

Practice Exercises

Instruction: Use this exercise to deepen your understanding of the lesson after reviewing each body part, such as the Adam's Apple or zygote, or after completing all the body parts in a particular letter set—A, B, or Z.

Task 1: Tagging Dialogues: Identify and list the dialogue tags used in the examples.

Task 2: Tracking Action Beats: Analyze the provided examples and identify action beats.

Task 3: Teasing Out Narrative Styles: Review the examples and distinguish between two narrative styles. Mark instances of deep POV that immerse you in a character's emotions or thoughts with a check mark (✓). Use an asterisk (*) to denote shallow POV instances, which focus primarily on surface-level actions or descriptions.

Task 4: Testing Your Skills with New Examples: Write four new phrases or short paragraphs incorporating an action beat and a dialogue tag. Use deep and shallow POV to explore different aspects of the body part discussed in this section.

Diaphragm

The diaphragm is a dome-shaped sheet of skeletal muscle that separates the chest cavity (thorax) from the abdominal cavity. It plays a crucial role in respiration (breathing).

Points of View

1. "I can't seem to catch my breath," I said to my doctor. "What can I do to strengthen my diaphragm?"
2. "I was struggling to breathe, and the pain around my diaphragm was unbearable," he explained to the paramedics.
3. "I'm practicing breathing exercises to improve my singing," she told her vocal coach. "My diaphragm feels stronger already."
4. "I've been coughing a lot, and now I'm feeling pain in my diaphragm," I told my friend. "I think I need to rest for a bit."
5. "Playing the trumpet for hours can really take a toll on the diaphragm," he said to his bandmate. "But it's worth it for the music."
6. "It's amazing how the diaphragm works," she said to her biology class. "It's like a little dance that keeps us alive."
7. "When I'm anxious, I notice my breathing gets shallow," I explained to my therapist. "What can I do to relax my diaphragm?"
8. "Take a deep breath and feel your diaphragm expand," he instructed his yoga class. "Let all your worries float away."
9. "I feel like I can't get enough air," she told her doctor. "Is there something wrong with my diaphragm?"
10. "Yoga has been really helpful for strengthening my diaphragm," I said to my friend. "And it's so relaxing, too."
11. "I've been smoking for years, and I can feel the strain on my diaphragm," he told his doctor. "I'm ready to quit and get healthy."
12. "I'm so grateful for my diaphragm," she said to her friend. "Without it, I wouldn't be able to do all the things I love."

Practice Exercises

Instruction: Use this exercise to deepen your understanding of the lesson after reviewing each body part, such as the Adam's Apple or zygote, or after completing all the body parts in a particular letter set—A, B, or Z.

Task 1: Tagging Dialogues: Identify and list the dialogue tags used in the examples.

Task 2: Tracking Action Beats: Analyze the provided examples and identify action beats.

Task 3: Teasing Out Narrative Styles: Review the examples and distinguish between two narrative styles. Mark instances of deep POV that immerse you in a character's emotions or thoughts with a check mark (✓). Use an asterisk (*) to denote shallow POV instances, which focus primarily on surface-level actions or descriptions.

Task 4: Testing Your Skills with New Examples: Write four new phrases or short paragraphs incorporating an action beat and a dialogue tag. Use deep and shallow POV to explore different aspects of the body part discussed in this section.

Ears

Located on either side of the head. They are parts of the body that detect vibrations in the air and convert them into signals that the brain interprets as sound. This process enables us to hear and interact with our environment.

Points of View

1. I heard a beautiful song in my ears and couldn't help but dance along to the rhythm.
2. My ears rang after a loud explosion, and I struggled to regain my hearing.
3. My ears perked up at the sound of my favorite artist's voice and I turned up the volume.
4. My ears were cold from the winter chill and I pulled my beanie down to cover them.
5. I felt embarrassed as my ears turned red during my public speaking engagement.
6. My ears were sensitive to high-pitched sounds and I cringed at the screeching of chalk on a blackboard.
7. My ears were blocked from a cold and I struggled to hear the conversation around me.
8. My ears picked up on the sound of rustling leaves and I knew that someone was approaching.
9. My ears twitched as I listened to the sounds of the forest, feeling at peace with nature.
10. My ears were pierced with multiple earrings, each with its own unique story and memory.
11. My ears were small and delicate, a feature that I always felt self-conscious about.
12. My ears were covered with noise-canceling headphones as I escaped into my own world of music.

Endometrium

The inner lining of the uterus that thickens every month. This is to prepare for the possibility of pregnancy, where it can support a developing baby.

Points of View

1. She imagined her endometrium as a welcoming bed prepared for a potential new life.
2. The endometrium was an unsung hero, silently preparing for a guest that might never arrive.
3. "Your endometrium is thickening nicely," the doctor reported, showing her the ultrasound.
4. She held her abdomen, thinking of the constant cycle her endometrium underwent.
5. Pain stabbed at her lower belly, a grim reminder of her endometrium shedding its hopeful lining.
6. The endometrium was like a patient landlord, preparing and repairing in a constant cycle.
7. "The endometrium thickens during the menstrual cycle," he explained, pointing to the chart.
8. She nodded, trying to comprehend the role of the endometrium in her fertility journey.
9. She could feel the twinges in her uterus, picturing her endometrium building its monthly nest.
10. The role of the endometrium was an awe-inspiring testament to the body's preparation for potential life.
11. "The endometrium can cause pain if it grows outside the uterus," the doctor explained.
12. He furrowed his brow, studying the information about endometrium for his upcoming test.

Epididymis

A coiled tube located behind each testicle. It stores sperm and helps carry them out of the testicles.

Points of View

1. I didn't know much about the epididymis, but I knew it played a role in male reproductive health. "What exactly does the epididymis do?" I asked my doctor.
2. My partner had a swollen epididymis, and I offered my support as he went through treatment. "I'm here for you," I told him.
3. My brother had a painful lump in his epididymis, and I accompanied him to the doctor for a diagnosis. "How are you feeling?" I asked him.
4. I read up on the anatomy of the male reproductive system, including the function of the epididymis. "It's fascinating how the male reproductive system works," I said to myself.
5. My father shared his experiences with a painful epididymis and how he coped with the discomfort. "It was tough, but I got through it," he told me.
6. My partner was self-conscious about the size of his epididymis, and I reassured him that it was normal. "Size doesn't matter," I said with a smile.
7. I learned about the potential causes of epididymitis, including STIs and other infections. "It's important to take care of your sexual health," my doctor told me.
8. I discussed the importance of regular check-ups and screenings for epididymal health with my partner. "We should make sure we're both healthy," I said to him.
9. My male friends joked about the sensitivity of their epididymis, but I knew it was a serious matter. "It's important to take care of your reproductive health," I told them.

10. I listened to a podcast on male reproductive health and learned about the functions of the epididymis in sperm maturation. "It's amazing how the body works," I thought to myself.
11. My partner had a congenital abnormality in his epididymis, and we had to make difficult decisions about our fertility options. "We'll get through this together," I told him.
12. I admired the resilience of the epididymis, a small but important part of the male reproductive system. "It's amazing how our bodies can adapt," I marveled.

Esophagus

A muscular tube that acts as a passageway between the mouth and stomach. It helps transport food and liquids safely and efficiently to the stomach during swallowing.

Points of View

1. I felt a lump in my esophagus and struggled to swallow my food. "Something's not right," I said to myself.
2. My grandmother had a condition that caused her esophagus to narrow, and she had to be careful with her diet. "I miss eating spicy food," she lamented.
3. My doctor recommended a scope to examine my esophagus for any signs of damage. "We need to figure out what's causing this," my doctor told me.
4. My sister suffered from acid reflux, which caused inflammation and discomfort in her esophagus. "I hate this burning feeling," she complained.
5. My mother choked on a piece of food that got stuck in her esophagus, and we had to call 911 for help. "I couldn't breathe," she gasped.
6. My uncle had to have surgery to repair a tear in his esophagus after a car accident. "I'm so glad I made it out alive," he said.
7. I avoided spicy and acidic foods to prevent irritation in my esophagus. "I'll stick to bland food for now," I told myself.
8. My friend was diagnosed with esophageal cancer, and I supported her throughout her treatment. "I'm scared," she confided in me.
9. I took a sip of hot coffee and felt the warmth spread down my esophagus. "Ah, that's soothing," I said with relief.
10. I had a phobia of swallowing pills and had to find alternative ways to take my medication. "I hate taking pills," I groaned.

11. My mother had a congenital abnormality in her esophagus that required specialized medical care. "It's been a lifelong struggle," she told me.

12. My friend had a condition that caused spasms in her esophagus, making it difficult to eat and drink. "I wish there was a cure for this," she said sadly.

Eyebrows

The hair strips above the eyes that help protect the eyes from sweat, water, and other debris. They also play a significant role in facial expressions, communicating emotions such as surprise, concern, and curiosity.

Points of View

1. Marah raised her eyebrows, a slight grin playing at the corners of her mouth as she explained to her curious niece. "You see, eyebrows aren't just there for looks. They actually help keep sweat and water from dripping into our eyes." She gestured to her own, running a finger just above one to demonstrate. "They channel all that annoying stuff away to the sides of our faces. Plus, they help us show how we feel without even saying a word, like this!" Her eyebrows shot up in exaggerated surprise, causing her niece to giggle.
2. Fifi's eyebrows arched in surprise when she received an unexpected gift.
3. Marah's eyebrows were unruly and she had to groom them regularly to keep them neat.
4. Fifi's eyebrows were thin and delicate, a feature that she loved about herself.
5. Marah's eyebrows twitched when she was nervous, a habit that she couldn't control.
6. Fifi's eyebrows were dark and defined, framing her face beautifully.
7. Marah's eyebrows raised in disbelief as she heard an outrageous claim.
8. Fifi's eyebrows were shaped into a perfect arch for a special occasion.
9. Marah's eyebrows were asymmetrical, and she often felt self-conscious about it.

10. Fifi's eyebrows had a scar from a childhood injury, a reminder of her adventurous spirit.
11. Marah's eyebrows had a few gray hairs, a sign of aging that she tried to hide with makeup.
12. Fifi's eyebrows were a prominent feature that often drew compliments from others.

Eyelashes

The short hairs that grow from the edges of the eyelids, which help protect the eyes from debris such as dust and sand. They also play a role in signaling when the eyelid needs to close reflexively to safeguard the eye.

Points of View

1. My eyelashes were so long that they would often get caught in my glasses.
2. Sage admired Rylan's eyelashes and wished she had longer ones.
3. The wind was so strong that it made my eyelashes flutter uncontrollably.
4. Rylan blinked rapidly, trying to get an eyelash out of her eye.
5. Sage was embarrassed when a stray eyelash fell onto her cheek during an important meeting.
6. Rylan's mascara clumped together, causing her eyelashes to stick together.
7. Sage plucked out a stray eyelash, making a wish as she blew it away.
8. Rylan leaned in, his voice a conspiratorial murmur that tickled my ear. "Eyelashes," he began, his eyes crinkling at the corners, "they're like tiny shields, you know?" He tapped his eyelid lightly, the sound echoing in the sudden quiet. "They catch dust and sand before it tickles your eyeballs, right?" He blinked slowly, a playful glint in his eyes. "And if something brushes them..." He paused for effect, then batted his lashes with a dramatic flourish. "Bam! Eyes blink on their own like magic! Pretty cool, huh?"
9. Sage's eyelashes were naturally curly, making it difficult to apply mascara evenly.
10. Rylan was jealous of Sage's thick and voluminous eyelashes.

11. Sage's eyelashes protected her eyes from getting dirt in them while hiking.
12. Rylan used an eyelash curler to enhance her eyelashes before a night out.

Eyelids

The movable folds of skin that cover the eyes. They protect the eyes from debris and help keep them moist by spreading tears evenly when you blink.

Points of View

1. My eyelids drooped with exhaustion after a long day at work.
2. Sage's eyelids were heavy with sleep as she struggled to keep them open.
3. Rylan's eyelids twitched nervously before a big presentation.
4. I rubbed my eyelids, trying to alleviate the strain from staring at a computer screen all day.
5. Sage's eyelids were puffy and red from crying all night.
6. Rylan's eyelids were sensitive to the touch after she accidentally got shampoo in her eyes.
7. My eyelids felt like they were glued shut after a nap.
8. Sage's eyelids were irritated from wearing contact lenses all day.
9. Rylan's eyelids fluttered when she was nervous or anxious.
10. I used my fingers to prop open my eyelids during a long lecture.
11. Sage's eyelids felt heavy with anticipation before a surprise birthday party.
12. Rylan's eyelids felt dry and itchy after forgetting to remove her makeup before bed.

Eyes

The organs of sight. They detect light and help us recognize shapes, colors, and where things are located.

Points of View

1. My eyes widened with surprise when I saw the birthday cake.
2. Sage's eyes sparkled with excitement when she saw her favorite musician on stage.
3. Rylan's eyes filled with tears of joy when she was proposed to.
4. I squinted my eyes, trying to see something in the distance.
5. Sage's eyes were the color of the ocean, and many people complimented her on them.
6. Rylan's eyes were a warm brown, and she often used them to convey emotion.
7. My eyes were red and bloodshot from lack of sleep.
8. Sage's eyes darted back and forth as she tried to solve a difficult math problem.
9. Rylan's eyes were sensitive to bright light and she always wore sunglasses outside.
10. I rubbed my eyes, trying to focus better after reading for a long time.
11. I blink rapidly, trying to clear my vision after being hit by a gust of wind.
12. I averted my eyes, feeling guilty for accidentally overhearing my friend's private conversation.

Practice Exercises

Instruction: Use this exercise to deepen your understanding of the lesson after reviewing each body part, such as the Adam's Apple or zygote, or after completing all the body parts in a particular letter set—A, B, or Z.

Task 1: Tagging Dialogues: Identify and list the dialogue tags used in the examples.

Task 2: Tracking Action Beats: Analyze the provided examples and identify action beats.

Task 3: Teasing Out Narrative Styles: Review the examples and distinguish between two narrative styles. Mark instances of deep POV that immerse you in a character's emotions or thoughts with a check mark (✓). Use an asterisk (*) to denote shallow POV instances, which focus primarily on surface-level actions or descriptions.

Task 4: Testing Your Skills with New Examples: Write four new phrases or short paragraphs incorporating an action beat and a dialogue tag. Use deep and shallow POV to explore different aspects of the body part discussed in this section.

Face

The front part of the head that extends from the forehead to the chin. It includes features such as the eyes, nose, and mouth.

Points of View

1. Seeing my best friend's face, something warm and familiar, I feel a smile tug at my lips. It's like coming home.
2. My reflection startles me. The toll of a sleepless night is etched into my face, and a cringe escapes before I can stop it.
3. Tears threaten, but I fight them back, my jaw clenching, my face a mask of strain. I won't let them see me break.
4. My siblings' antics are just ridiculous. I can't help but roll my eyes, yet a spark of amusement dances across my face. They never change.
5. A gasp escapes her lips as a stranger's face comes into view.
6. He furrows his brow, his face filled with confusion as he tries to solve the problem.
7. A sense of peace washes over her face as she closes her eyes to meditate.
8. Warmth spreads across my face as my cheeks flush. Our eyes meet – my crush's and mine – and I'm caught, breathless.
9. My lips purse, every line of my face taut with concentration. This task demands everything, and I lose myself in it.
10. A grin spreads across his face as he watches his favorite movie.
11. Her face falls into a frown as she reads the rejection letter, disappointment clear.
12. His teeth are gritted, and determination shows on his face as he powers through a tough workout.

Fallopian tubes

Also known as oviducts: These are the two thin tubes, each connecting an ovary to the uterus in females. They act as pathways for eggs to travel from the ovaries, where fertilization by sperm typically occurs, facilitating the possibility of pregnancy.

Points of View

1. I feel a twinge of pain as my ovary releases an egg into my fallopian tube.
2. I cross my legs protectively as I think of the delicate fallopian tubes within me.
3. I tense up as the doctor discusses the possibility of a blockage in my fallopian tubes.
4. I feel a sense of hope as the fertility specialist mentions the possibility of unblocking my fallopian tubes.
5. I cringe at the thought of an ectopic pregnancy, where the fertilized egg implants in the fallopian tube instead of the uterus.
6. I breathe a sigh of relief as the ultrasound shows my healthy, open fallopian tubes.
7. I feel a sense of awe as I learn about the intricate functions of my fallopian tubes in creating life.
8. I squirm uncomfortably as I undergo a hysterosalpingogram to check for blockages in my fallopian tubes.
9. I feel a sense of loss as I learn that one of my fallopian tubes has to be removed due to a medical issue.
10. I clench my fists as I listen to ignorant comments about the function of fallopian tubes from someone who doesn't understand reproductive health.
11. I feel a sense of gratitude for my fallopian tubes as I hold my newborn baby in my arms.
12. I cradle my belly protectively, aware of the precious cargo growing within my fallopian tubes.

Feet

The feet are the lower extremities of the legs, located below the ankles. Made up of various bones, joints, muscles, tendons, and ligaments, they play a vital role in supporting the body's weight and facilitating movement.

Points of View

1. The cold tile sends a shiver through Fifi's feet. "Ugh," she cringes, stepping back quickly. "I hate the feeling of cold feet."
2. Adinah sighs in relief, slipping off her high heels. "Finally," she says, flexing her toes, "my feet can breathe."
3. "Ew!" Adinah exclaims, squirming as her socks soak through. "I hate when my feet get wet."
4. A jolt of pain shot up Marah's feet, eliciting a startled yelp. Hopping on one foot, then the other, she winced, unsure which offender to coddle first. "Seriously? Why do I always do this to you?"
5. The fresh ocean air fills Adinah's lungs as she kicks off her flip-flops. Her feet meet the water, and she breathes a contented sigh, "Ahh."
6. "Mmm," Adinah murmurs, curling her toes under the covers. "It's so cozy in bed; I don't want to leave." Her feet feel warm and snug.
7. Fifi stretches her feet out, feeling the cool grass beneath her soles. She sighs contentedly, her eyes closing for a moment. "There's nothing like being barefoot in the garden," she says, happiness in her voice. "I could spend hours just feeling the earth between my toes."
8. The tension in Adinah's feet finally releases as she stretches them out. "Ahh," she sighs, relief washing over her after the long car ride.

9. Fifi balances on her tiptoes, her feet straining. "Just a little higher," she says, reaching for China wares on a high shelf.

10. "I love the freedom of bare feet," Marah exclaims, joyfully pulling off her socks, the fresh air enveloping her feet.

11. The carpet is soft and cozy beneath Marah's feet. She moves her toes, enjoying the sensation. "This carpet feels amazing," she comments, comfort in every word.

12. Adinah wiggles her feet in the sand, a smile spreading across her face. "This is the life," she declares. "I could stay here forever."

Fingers

The digits on the hands used for grasping and manipulating objects. They play a role in various activities, from writing to holding tools.

Points of View

1. I rubbed my fingers together nervously as I waited for her to speak.
2. She drummed her fingers on the table impatiently, clearly annoyed with the situation.
3. I couldn't help but feel a shiver run down my spine as she traced her fingers lightly over my skin.
4. "Can you believe how fast she types?" I asked, watching her fingers fly over the keyboard with impressive speed.
5. She winced in pain as I accidentally stepped on her fingers.
6. I felt a sense of pride swell within me as I watched her deftly play the piano with her slender fingers.
7. "Can you help me open this jar?" she asked, struggling with the lid as she grabbed it with her fingers.
8. The cold winter air made my fingers numb as I fumbled with the keys in the lock.
9. I clenched my fingers into fists, trying to control my anger and frustration.
10. She twirled her hair around her fingers absentmindedly as we talked.
11. My heart skipped a beat as she brushed her fingers against mine.
12. "Stop biting your nails," she scolded, eyeing my bitten fingers disapprovingly.

Fingernails

The hard, protective coverings at each finger's tips. They help protect the sensitive tips from injuries and can also be used for picking up or manipulating small objects.

Points of View

1. I stare at my fingernails, admiring the glossy pink polish I just applied.
2. I bite my fingernails nervously as I wait for the phone to ring.
3. My fingernails scrape against the chalkboard, sending shivers down my spine.
4. I pick at my fingernail, trying to remove a speck of dirt stuck underneath.
5. I drum my fingernails against the tabletop, impatiently waiting for the meeting to start.
6. I examine my broken fingernail, wincing at the pain.
7. I trace the outline of the heart on the notepad with my fingernail, lost in thought.
8. I tap my fingernails against the steering wheel, singing along to the radio.
9. I used my fingernail to scratch the mosquito bite on my arm.
10. I run my fingernail along the edge of the envelope, feeling the texture of the paper.
11. I press my fingernail into the soft clay, shaping it into a tiny figurine.
12. I clenched my fist, digging my fingernails into my palm to control my anger.

Foot

The foot is the lower extremity of the leg, located below the ankle, and comprises various bones, joints, muscles, tendons, and ligaments. It includes parts such as the ankle, heel, sole, and toes and plays a vital role in supporting the body's weight and facilitating movement.

Points of View

1. My right foot aches with every step, a throbbing reminder of the long hike. I stumble, gritting my teeth against the pain, but I'm determined to keep moving forward.
2. "Ouch! I think I hurt my foot," he winces, grabbing his ankle. "This hike is getting rough."
3. "I can't believe I stepped on a nail with my bare right foot!" she exclaimed, cradling her foot. "This is the last thing I needed today."
4. The soft sand feels luxurious beneath my tender left foot, the waves lapping gently at my toes. I sigh contentedly, letting the stress melt away.
5. "I never realized how much I needed my right foot until I broke it," he sighed. "Even simple tasks like walking are now so difficult."
6. A sudden, searing pain shoots up my left foot! I cry out and look down to find a bee sting, the realization only amplifying the throbbing pain.
7. "I think there's something stuck in my right foot," she said with a slight limp. "Can you take a look?"
8. The foot massage feels incredible. Each kneading and press send waves of relaxation through my entire right leg. I melt into the chair, utterly content.
9. "Ugh, a pebble in my shoe!" she exclaims, pulling it off and shaking it out.

10. "Watch out for that puddle!" he yelled, but it was too late. My left foot splashes into the cold water, and I can't help but laugh at my own clumsiness.

11. Balancing on my right foot, I focus all my energy on maintaining the yoga pose. With slow breaths in and out, I find a moment of clarity and peace.

12. "Keep your left foot elevated and apply some ice," the doctor instructed. I nod, relief washing over me as the hope of recovery dawns.

Forehead

The part of the face that extends above the eyes and up to the hairline. This area is prominent and often used for expressing emotions through movements such as frowning or raising eyebrows.

Points of View

1. I furrowed my forehead in concentration, trying to solve the puzzle in front of me.
2. She pressed her forehead against mine, sharing an intimate moment.
3. "I can't believe I forgot my keys again," I groaned, slapping my forehead with my hand.
4. I wiped the sweat from my forehead with the back of my hand, feeling exhausted after the intense workout.
5. She wrinkled her forehead in confusion, trying to understand the complex instructions.
6. "Don't worry, everything will be okay," she said, placing a reassuring hand on my forehead.
7. I winced in pain as I accidentally bumped my forehead against the low-hanging branch.
8. She leaned her forehead against the cool glass of the window, watching the rain pour down.
9. I couldn't help but feel a sense of relief wash over me as the doctor checked my forehead for a fever and declared me healthy.
10. "Why are you so stressed out?" she asked, noticing the deep lines etched into my forehead.
11. I felt a sense of pride swell within me as I watched my child receive her diploma and cross the stage, a huge grin spreading across her face, reaching to her forehead.
12. I felt my forehead flush with embarrassment as I realized my mistake in front of everyone.

Practice Exercises

Instruction: Use this exercise to deepen your understanding of the lesson after reviewing each body part, such as the Adam's Apple or zygote, or after completing all the body parts in a particular letter set—A, B, or Z.

Task 1: Tagging Dialogues: Identify and list the dialogue tags used in the examples.

Task 2: Tracking Action Beats: Analyze the provided examples and identify action beats.

Task 3: Teasing Out Narrative Styles: Review the examples and distinguish between two narrative styles. Mark instances of deep POV that immerse you in a character's emotions or thoughts with a check mark (✓). Use an asterisk (*) to denote shallow POV instances, which focus primarily on surface-level actions or descriptions.

Task 4: Testing Your Skills with New Examples: Write four new phrases or short paragraphs incorporating an action beat and a dialogue tag. Use deep and shallow POV to explore different aspects of the body part discussed in this section.

Gallbladder

A small, pear-shaped organ located under the liver. It stores bile, a fluid produced by the liver, and releases it into the small intestine. This process allows the absorption of fat-soluble vitamins and the efficient digestion of dietary fats.

Points of View

1. "Ouch! My gallbladder is acting up again."
2. A sinking feeling washed over me at the realization of having to bid farewell to my gallbladder.
3. The pain, a ruthless tormentor residing in my gallbladder, is becoming unbearable.
4. Each meal has turned into a strategic game, navigating around foods that trigger gallbladder attacks.
5. The doctor's words echoed in my mind: "Your gallbladder is a rock garden."
6. The gallbladder pain, like a master puppeteer, yanked strings that stretched into my back.
7. A wave of nausea crashed over me, bloating my confidence – it had to be the gallbladder again.
8. My gallbladder pain became an unwelcome gatecrasher, forcing me to abandon work.
9. Hope, a fragile bird in my chest, fluttered at the thought of the impending gallbladder surgery.
10. I yearned for a natural remedy, a magic wand to banish my gallbladder issues.
11. Fatty foods have turned traitor, exacerbating the pain in my gallbladder.
12. "I can't wait to feel better after my gallbladder surgery."

Gluteal muscles

The muscles in the buttocks that are responsible for moving the hips and thighs. They assist in maintaining posture and provide support while standing or sitting, enhancing balance and mobility.

Points of View

1. "I can barely sit down; my gluteal muscles are so sore," groaned Alex after yesterday's workout.
2. "I always make sure to stretch my gluteal muscles before exercising," said Sage, demonstrating a stretch.
3. "I've been working hard to strengthen my gluteal muscles and it's paying off," boasted Rylan.
4. "Out of all the muscle groups, my favorite to work on is definitely my gluteal muscles," said Alex with a smile.
5. "I've been feeling a knot in my gluteal muscles for days – it's so uncomfortable," complained Rylan.
6. "I want to improve my posture, so I need to focus on strengthening my gluteal muscles," stated Sage.
7. "I booked a massage to relieve the tension in my gluteal muscles," announced Avery.
8. "After sitting for hours, my gluteal muscles are cramping up," winced Sage.
9. "Nothing beats doing squats to target my gluteal muscles," said Fifi, demonstrating perfect form.
10. "After my long run, my gluteal muscles ache so much," sighed Shaquille.
11. "My gluteal muscles are getting toned from my workouts, but I still have cellulite," admitted Marah with frustration.
12. "I need to switch up my routine and incorporate more exercises to target my gluteal muscles," mused Adinah.

Practice Exercises

Instruction: Use this exercise to deepen your understanding of the lesson after reviewing each body part, such as the Adam's Apple or zygote, or after completing all the body parts in a particular letter set—A, B, or Z.

Task 1: Tagging Dialogues: Identify and list the dialogue tags used in the examples.

Task 2: Tracking Action Beats: Analyze the provided examples and identify action beats.

Task 3: Teasing Out Narrative Styles: Review the examples and distinguish between two narrative styles. Mark instances of deep POV that immerse you in a character's emotions or thoughts with a check mark (✓). Use an asterisk (*) to denote shallow POV instances, which focus primarily on surface-level actions or descriptions.

Task 4: Testing Your Skills with New Examples: Write four new phrases or short paragraphs incorporating an action beat and a dialogue tag. Use deep and shallow POV to explore different aspects of the body part discussed in this section.

Hair

A protein filament that grows from follicles found in the dermis, or skin. They can be found all over our bodies, not just on our heads. The color, thickness, and length of hair can vary a lot from person to person.

Points of View

1. "Something is soothing about the way the breeze teases the hair on my arms when I hike," she mused, tracing a line down her arm with her fingers.
2. "Great, the hair on my legs is already growing back," she grumbled, her gaze cast down to the tiny dark spots reappearing on her skin.
3. She ran a fingertip along her brow, feeling the individual hairs. "I've stopped trimming my eyebrows, I kind of like this natural look."
4. He glanced at his reflection, his chest hair appearing darker and more pronounced. "Might be time to try that waxing idea," he murmured apprehensively.
5. A sigh escaped him as he rubbed the edge of his nose. "Didn't think plucking nose hair would take this long."
6. A daring glint sparked in her eyes as she looked in the mirror. "Dyeing my armpit hair could be fun," she murmured with a grin.
7. Her gaze traveled down her arms, the hair there seemingly more noticeable. "I wish it was less obvious," she admitted quietly.
8. "I didn't think I'd feel this self-conscious about losing hair on my arms," he confessed, tugging his sleeve down to cover his bare skin.
9. "We're a family who embraces our body hair, a tradition I'm proud of," she declared, her hand brushing over her unshaven leg.

10. His hand froze halfway to his face, feeling the bare patch on his cheek. "How did I manage to shave off a chunk of my hair?" he groaned.
11. Her hand swept over her smooth scalp, the sensation still new and pleasantly cool. "Who knew having my hair shaved could feel this refreshing?"
12. "Why does my facial hair have to be so coarse?" he groused, fingers rasping over the stubble on his chin with annoyance.

Hand

The body parts located at the end of the arms, consisting of the palm, fingers, and thumb. The hands perform a wide range of tasks, from grasping and holding to manipulating objects and performing delicate movements.

Points of View

1. "I love the feel of my newborn baby's tiny hand wrapped around my finger," she gushed, holding the little hand.
2. "This hangnail on my left hand is awful! It's driving me nuts!" she exclaimed, picking at it relentlessly. It is central to many functions, including thinking, seeing, hearing, smelling, and tasting.
3. "I have a terrible hangnail that's driving me crazy," she complained, picking at her finger.
4. "I got a splinter in my hand from that old fence," he grumbled, examining the palm of his hand.
5. "I wish I had a steady hand like my sister. She's an amazing artist," she admired, watching her sibling sketch.
6. "I'm so clumsy, I always manage to burn my hand on the stove," he chuckled, showing off a bandaged finger.
7. "I can't believe how much my hands are shaking after that intense workout," she panted, holding her palms out.
8. The warmth of the cup seeped into her hands, the gentle heat providing solace on a bitterly cold day. As she lifted the tea to her lips, her heart found its smile.
9. He held up his hand, proudly displaying a knot of intricate design. His fingers had danced around the rope, expertly maneuvering it into a complex pattern. The ability was a badge of honor to him, a testament to his nimble hands.

10. She squinted at the elusive eye of the needle, her hand wavering despite her best efforts. The thread grazed the hole, yet slipped away time and again, her shaky hands betraying her.

11. She cast a regretful look at her bitten-down nails. Despite her many attempts to stop, her hands seemed to have a mind of their own, perpetually finding their way to her mouth.

12. He traced the aged scar on his hand with a nostalgic smile. Each rough line was a reminder of his biking mishap, a memento of youthful fearlessness etched into his skin.

Head

The upper part of the body that houses sensory organs such as the brain, eyes, ears, nose, and mouth.

Points of View

1. My head aches terribly, I need to rest a while," Jesus groaned, holding his temples.
2. "I have an exceptional memory; I can recall every detail of that event," Jesus boasted, tapping his head.
3. Jesus's brows drew together, his head bent over the open notebook. His memory often failed him, but his trusty lists never did; they were the anchors in his forgetful world.
4. A challenging puzzle lay scattered before Jesus. His head hummed with anticipation, every piece a mystery to solve, each connection a victory in this cerebral game he relished.
5. Jesus shook his head, his mind whirling like a cyclone with the shocking news. He struggled to comprehend, his head a whirlpool of disbelief.
6. Pain drummed a merciless beat in Jesus's head. He cupped his aching head in his hands, yearning for a moment of silence, a reprieve from the relentless throbbing.
7. A fresh start. That's what Jesus envisaged as he decided to shave his head. It wasn't just about appearance, but a symbol of renewal. His head, now bare, was a testament to his bold new beginning.
8. The stubborn tune wound its way around Jesus's head, refusing to leave. It played on a constant loop, a distraction he didn't need, making concentration a challenging task.
9. Jesus invited closeness, the sensation of another's head resting on his shoulder stirring joy within him. The intimate touch was soothing, a comfort that he quietly cherished.

10. Jesus's head throbbed as he raked his fingers through his hair in frustration. His belongings had a way of disappearing, turning him into an unwilling detective in his own life, a game that was growing old.
11. The spinning is making my head throb! Fun, but definitely disorienting," Jesus giggled as they danced around the room.
12. "I hit my head on that low-hanging branch and it hurts," Jesus groaned, rubbing the sore spot.

Heart

The muscular organ in the chest that pumps blood throughout the body via the circulatory system. It continuously circulates oxygen and nutrients to tissues and removes carbon dioxide and other wastes.

Points of View

1. "My heart is racing with excitement, I can't wait to see what's inside," she whispered, as she opened the beautifully wrapped gift.
2. "I feel like my heart is breaking into a million pieces," she cried, as she heard the news of her grandfather's passing.
3. "My heart swells with pride whenever I see my son's accomplishments," she beamed, watching him receive his diploma.
4. "I know in my heart that I can make a difference," she declared, determined to pursue her dreams.
5. "My heart skips a beat every time I see him," she blushed, as she caught sight of her crush.
6. "I feel a heaviness in my heart whenever I think about the past," she sighed, reflecting on her mistakes.
7. "My heart is filled with gratitude for all the blessings in my life," she said, as she gave thanks for her loved ones.
8. "I can feel my heart pounding in my chest, like a drumbeat," she gasped, after she ran the marathon.
9. "My heart aches with longing for a love that's out of reach," she mused, staring out at the starry sky.
10. "I feel my heart racing with fear, like a wild animal trying to escape," she whispered, as she prepared to give her speech.
11. "My heart feels light and free when I dance," she smiled, swaying to the rhythm of the music.
12. "I can feel my heart overflowing with love for my newborn baby," she cried, cradling the tiny bundle in her arms.

Heels

The back part of a person's foot below the ankle. This prominent area forms the rear base of the foot, providing support and balance when standing or walking.

Points of View

1. These new shoes make me feel like I'm walking on clouds," she giggled, admiring her high heels. "How fitting," Lucifer remarked, a hint of amusement in his voice.
2. "My heels are killing me from standing all day," she groaned, massaging her sore feet. "Punishment for vanity, perhaps," Lucifer remarked dryly.
3. "I love the sound of my heels clicking on the pavement," she smiled, as she strutted down the street. "Such a shame it announces your arrival," Lucifer remarked, his tone dripping with sarcasm.
4. "My heels are slipping on the ice, I need to be careful," she warned, shuffling her feet cautiously. "Fear not, my dear," Lucifer reassured her. "I'll catch you if you fall."
5. "I feel like a queen in these heels, towering over everyone else," she boasted, standing tall. "Queens are often dethroned," Lucifer reminded her, his voice laced with warning.
6. "My heels are sinking into the sand at the beach," she laughed, feeling the grains tickle her toes. "Enjoy it while it lasts," Lucifer said, his tone tinged with melancholy.
7. "I can't wear heels for too long, they make my feet ache," she complained, switching to comfortable flats. "The pain of beauty," Lucifer mused, a sly grin on his face.
8. "I feel like a spy in these secret agent heels," she joked, admiring the hidden compartments. "Secrets are a double-edged sword," Lucifer warned, his voice low and dangerous.

9. "My heels are stuck in this cobblestone street, I need to pull them out," she grumbled, yanking on her shoes. "Patience, my dear," Lucifer said soothingly. "You'll get out eventually."

10. "I love the way my heels elongate my legs and make me feel confident," she admired, striking a pose. "Confidence can be a fatal flaw," Lucifer cautioned, his voice laced with malice.

11. "My heels are slipping off my feet, I need to adjust the straps," she frowned, tightening the buckles. "Vanity demands sacrifice," Lucifer remarked, a hint of amusement in his voice.

12. "I can't resist the urge to tap my heels together like Dorothy in *The Wizard of Oz*," she smiled, reliving a childhood memory. "Ah, the power of magic," Lucifer said, his voice low and hypnotic.

Hip

The area on either side of the body where the upper part of the pelvis meets the upper end of the thigh bone, forming the hip joint. This joint supports the body's weight and enables movements like walking and sitting.

Points of View

1. "I can feel my hips swaying to the rhythm of the music," Missy said, her eyes closed in ecstasy.
2. "My hips ache after that intense workout, but it's worth it for the gains," she said, gritting her teeth through the pain.
3. "I love the way my hips look in this dress, it makes me feel confident and sexy," she said, admiring her reflection with a smile.
4. "I can't believe I slipped on that wet floor and landed on my hip. It hurts so much," Missy groaned, clutching the injured area tightly.
5. "My hips don't lie – they're telling me to keep dancing," she laughed, her body moving to the beat.
6. "I'm so glad I started doing yoga; it's really helped loosen up my hips," she said, stretching into a pose with a satisfied sigh.
7. "I hate how society puts so much pressure on women to have a certain hip size," Missy said, her frustration palpable.
8. "I feel like I have to constantly wiggle my hips to keep up with the latest dance moves," she joked, practicing her steps with a grin.
9. "My hips are my secret weapon on the dance floor, they always steal the show," she grinned, showing off her moves with pride.
10. "I'm always self-conscious about my hips when I wear tight jeans, but sometimes you just have to embrace your curves," she said, feeling empowered.
11. "I can't wait to get back to salsa dancing – it's all about the hips," she said, excitement bubbling up in her voice.
12. "I love the way my boyfriend's hands feel on my hips when we dance cheek to cheek," Missy blushed, reliving a special moment with a dreamy look in her eyes.

Hypothalamus

A small but critical area of the brain that regulates essential bodily functions such as hunger, thirst, body temperature, and sleep patterns. It serves as a control center, linking the nervous system to the endocrine system through the pituitary gland, helping maintain overall body balance.

Points of View

1. "My hypothalamus is making me feel so hungry, but I'm trying to resist the urge to snack," she grumbled, struggling with her diet.
2. "I wish I could control my hypothalamus; it's the reason I can't sleep properly at night," he sighed, frustrated with his insomnia.
3. "My hypothalamus is telling me that I'm in love with him, but my logical brain knows better," she said, conflicted with her emotions.
4. "I hate how my hypothalamus always makes me crave junk food. It's so hard to resist," he groaned, trying to maintain a healthy lifestyle.
5. "I can feel my hypothalamus releasing stress hormones. I need to take a break and relax," she said, feeling overwhelmed.
6. "My hypothalamus is making my heart race, but I can't help feeling excited about this new opportunity," he said, with anticipation.
7. "I wish I could turn off my hypothalamus. It's the reason I get so anxious in social situations," she confessed, struggling with shyness.
8. "My hypothalamus is telling me that something is wrong. I need to trust my gut instinct," he said, sensing danger.

9. "I'm so grateful for my hypothalamus. It helps regulate my body temperature and keeps me healthy," she said, appreciating her physiology.

10. "My hypothalamus is making me feel so tired. I need to listen to my body and get some rest," he yawned, feeling exhausted.

11. "I can feel my hypothalamus releasing dopamine. This new hobby is really making me happy," she smiled, enjoying her passion.

12. "I hate how my hypothalamus always makes me feel so emotional during my period. It's such a rollercoaster," she grumbled, "dealing with PMS."

Practice Exercises

Instruction: Use this exercise to deepen your understanding of the lesson after reviewing each body part, such as the Adam's Apple or zygote, or after completing all the body parts in a particular letter set—A, B, or Z.

Task 1: Tagging Dialogues: Identify and list the dialogue tags used in the examples.

Task 2: Tracking Action Beats: Analyze the provided examples and identify action beats.

Task 3: Teasing Out Narrative Styles: Review the examples and distinguish between two narrative styles. Mark instances of deep POV that immerse you in a character's emotions or thoughts with a check mark (✓). Use an asterisk (*) to denote shallow POV instances, which focus primarily on surface-level actions or descriptions.

Task 4: Testing Your Skills with New Examples: Write four new phrases or short paragraphs incorporating an action beat and a dialogue tag. Use deep and shallow POV to explore different aspects of the body part discussed in this section.

Irises

The colored part of the eye surrounding the pupil. Irises control the amount of light that enters the eye by adjusting the pupil's size.

Points of View

1. Fear shot through Trixie as her irises dilated, giving away her terror.
2. His excitement was contagious, and Trixie couldn't help but grin as his irises sparkled.
3. As their irises locked, Trixie felt a jolt of recognition deep in her chest.
4. Trixie couldn't help but wonder if the suspect's odd irises had anything to do with the crime.
5. Trixie's green irises blinked rapidly, trying to shake off the bright lights of the interrogation room.
6. Trixie's heart raced as his irises darkened with fury.
7. As exhaustion took over, Trixie's irises fluttered closed, and she surrendered to sleep.
8. Trixie tried not to flinch as the doctor examined her irises with a magnifying glass.
9. The artist's meticulous brush strokes captured the intricacies of Trixie's irises in stunning detail.
10. Trixie's irises shimmered with unshed tears as she struggled to keep her emotions in check.
11. Confusion clouded Trixie's mind as his irises flickered with uncertainty.
12. She was mesmerized by the deep, rich hues of his irises, unable to look away.

Practice Exercises

Instruction: Use this exercise to deepen your understanding of the lesson after reviewing each body part, such as the Adam's Apple or zygote, or after completing all the body parts in a particular letter set—A, B, or Z.

Task 1: Tagging Dialogues: Identify and list the dialogue tags used in the examples.

Task 2: Tracking Action Beats: Analyze the provided examples and identify action beats.

Task 3: Teasing Out Narrative Styles: Review the examples and distinguish between two narrative styles. Mark instances of deep POV that immerse you in a character's emotions or thoughts with a check mark (✓). Use an asterisk (*) to denote shallow POV instances, which focus primarily on surface-level actions or descriptions.

Task 4: Testing Your Skills with New Examples: Write four new phrases or short paragraphs incorporating an action beat and a dialogue tag. Use deep and shallow POV to explore different aspects of the body part discussed in this section.

Jaw

The bone structure that forms the lower part of the skull, supports the mouth, holds the teeth, and aids in chewing and speaking.

Points of View

1. Anger bubbled within him, fighting for release, making his jaw clench.
2. Exhaustion etched into her being, concentrated in the throbbing soreness of her jaw.
3. Surprise coiled within him, dropping his jaw as the news bombarded his senses.
4. Pain scorched through her, originating from her gritted teeth and radiating outward through her jaw.
5. "He set his jaw stubbornly, determined not to give in."
6. Unshed tears stung her eyes, causing a reflexive tightening of her jaw.
7. "He leaned his jaw on his hand, lost in thought."
8. As she tilted her head back, her jaw opened wide in surrender to the approaching dentist's instruments.
9. Laughter rumbled within him, manifesting in the visible contractions of his jaw muscles.
10. Fear took her breath hostage, resulting in a reflexive clench of her jaw as the rollercoaster climbed higher.
11. Nervous anticipation made his jaw twitch, his mind spinning with what the results might reveal.
12. Frustration etched into her features, her lips pressed into a thin line, and the muscles in her jaws bunching noticeably.

Jawline

The contour of the lower jawbone, noted for the visible prominence of the chin and jaw. It defines the shape of the lower face and is a key element of facial aesthetics.

Points of View

1. Judas' reassurance came earnestly, a compliment that echoed his conviction. "You do not need contouring; your jawline is just perfect."
2. The compliment rolled off Judas' tongue, unabashed. "Even under that beard, your strong jawline is undeniable."
3. Teasingly, Judas noted the adorable twitch that betrayed an attempted suppression of laughter. "There's that jawline twitch, trying to hide a laugh?"
4. "The surgeon did an amazing job on your jawline. You look incredible." Judas praised.
5. "Your double chin doesn't detract from your beautiful jawline. It's just another feature that makes you unique," Judas encouraged.
6. "I admire how prominent your jawline is; it shows strength and confidence," Judas complimented.
7. "Your jawline is so smooth; it's like tracing a perfect curve," said Judas.
8. Awe filled Judas, and he could only manage a breathless "Wow." His gaze drifted upwards, landing on Rylan's striking jawline.
9. "Your jawline." Judas marveled; his words were inadequate to capture the striking impression it had on him.
10. Warm admiration filled Judas as he praised, "O, the way your jawline is defined. I love it."
11. Judas marveled at the mesmerizing sight. "The way the light hits your jawline. It's captivating.
12. A tender smile softened Judas' typically rigid jawline. Observing this, warmth blossomed in his chest, igniting a sense of secret intimacy.

Practice Exercises

Instruction: Use this exercise to deepen your understanding of the lesson after reviewing each body part, such as the Adam's Apple or zygote, or after completing all the body parts in a particular letter set—A, B, or Z.

Task 1: Tagging Dialogues: Identify and list the dialogue tags used in the examples.

Task 2: Tracking Action Beats: Analyze the provided examples and identify action beats.

Task 3: Teasing Out Narrative Styles: Review the examples and distinguish between two narrative styles. Mark instances of deep POV that immerse you in a character's emotions or thoughts with a check mark (✓). Use an asterisk (*) to denote shallow POV instances, which focus primarily on surface-level actions or descriptions.

Task 4: Testing Your Skills with New Examples: Write four new phrases or short paragraphs incorporating an action beat and a dialogue tag. Use deep and shallow POV to explore different aspects of the body part discussed in this section.

Kidneys

Two bean-shaped organs located below the rib cage, on either side of the spine. They act as a natural filter for the body, removing waste and excess water from the blood. This process helps maintain the body's chemical balance and produces urine.

Points of View

1. He winced, feeling a sharp pain in his kidneys.
2. She rubbed her lower back, feeling the strain on her kidneys.
3. His kidneys ached from the dehydration.
4. Gulping down water, she hoped the relentless flow would cleanse her aching kidneys.
5. He clenched his jaw, feeling the doctor's probing fingers against his tender kidneys.
6. A long, deep sigh escaped her lips as the vise-like pain in her kidneys began to subside.
7. "I'm afraid your kidneys have failed. You're going to need dialysis," the doctor's words rang out coldly. His world came crashing down around him as he faced the cold reality.
8. "Sorry, I need to step out for a moment," she excused herself, a familiar and uncomfortable urge tugging at her bladder to empty her kidneys.
9. A low groan escaped his lips as he felt an intense pressure bearing down on his kidneys after the heavy lift.
10. Her hands traveled to her lower back, kneading the tense muscles in a bid to ease the gnawing pain from her kidneys.
11. The medical report was a beacon of hope in his hand: his kidneys were functioning perfectly.
12. Sipping her herbal tea, she pondered if the earthy brew could indeed provide any real benefits to her kidneys.

Knees

The joints connecting the upper and lower legs. They help us bend and straighten our legs, allowing activities like walking, running, and jumping.

Points of View

1. An unexpected surge of pain shot through her knees as they collided with the unforgiving edge of the coffee table.
2. His knees, traitorous, trembled under the crushing weight of his fear.
3. She groaned, the slow circles she massaged into her tender knees doing little to alleviate the lingering ache from the strenuous hike.
4. Rising, the familiar pop in his knees rang out as he stretched, a silent reminder of the years that had slipped away.
5. She twisted abruptly, a sharp and sudden pain biting into her knees.
6. His knees buckled under the burden of his backpack, mocking his resolve.
7. Dropping to one knee, he pulled out the small velvet box, his voice soft but firm. "Will you marry me?"
8. She squealed, hopping up and down with unabashed glee, the spring in her knees matching the rhythm of her elation.
9. His knees gave a loud crack as he stooped to gather the fallen book.
10. "Your knees are perfectly healthy," the doctor assured her, and with those words, a wave of relief washed over her.
11. He grinned, knees creaking with each step but not diminishing his determination.
12. A pang of pain shot through her knee, causing her to wince.

Practice Exercises

Instruction: Use this exercise to deepen your understanding of the lesson after reviewing each body part, such as the Adam's Apple or zygote, or after completing all the body parts in a particular letter set—A, B, or Z.

Task 1: Tagging Dialogues: Identify and list the dialogue tags used in the examples.

Task 2: Tracking Action Beats: Analyze the provided examples and identify action beats.

Task 3: Teasing Out Narrative Styles: Review the examples and distinguish between two narrative styles. Mark instances of deep POV that immerse you in a character's emotions or thoughts with a check mark (✓). Use an asterisk (*) to denote shallow POV instances, which focus primarily on surface-level actions or descriptions.

Task 4: Testing Your Skills with New Examples: Write four new phrases or short paragraphs incorporating an action beat and a dialogue tag. Use deep and shallow POV to explore different aspects of the body part discussed in this section.

Large Intestine

Also known as the colon: A vital part of the digestive system that follows the small intestine. It absorbs water from digested food, which helps make the stool more solid. The large intestine also stores this waste until it is eliminated from the body.

Points of View

1. Marah leaned against the kitchen counter, swirling her tea with a spoon as she shared her newfound knowledge. "Our food travels like this," Marah said, sketching a line in the air. "Stomach, small intestine, large intestine." She paused, looking up to ensure her friend was following. "After the stomach does its work, the small intestine absorbs the nutrients. Whatever's left goes into the large intestine where it absorbs water before, well, you know, we get rid of it."

2. I'm struggling to find the right tone for this scene, much like how the large intestine faces challenges in its complex functions.

3. I'm carefully choosing my words, ensuring they work as effectively as the large intestine in absorbing what's essential.

4. I'm overwhelmed with all these ideas swirling around in my head. I need to filter them out, like the large intestine absorbing nutrients from food.

5. Feeling a slight cramp, she recognized the familiar discomfort in her lower abdomen, a subtle reminder of her large intestine's ongoing battle with the morning's coffee.

6. He paused, the sensation of bloating overwhelming his concentration as his large intestine struggled to process last night's heavy meal.

7. I can't believe how much editing this manuscript needs. It's like my large intestine is working overtime to eliminate all the unnecessary parts.

8. A sudden sharp pain during the meeting made him aware of his large intestine's distress, likely due to his stress.
9. She heard gurgling sounds from her abdomen at night, aware that her large intestine was slowly processing her food.
10. I must trust my instincts and let go of unnecessary details. Just like the large intestine knows what to absorb and what to eliminate.
11. I'm taking my time to polish this chapter, as the large intestine takes time to absorb all the nutrients from food. Quality over quantity.
12. "The large intestine is like the unsung hero of a carnival clean-up crew. Diligently working behind the scenes. It carefully sifts through the remains of the day's feast, reclaiming water and salts and packing up the leftovers into tidy little packages ready for their grand exit. It's a resourceful recycler, ensuring everything is neat and tidy before it all goes out!

Legs

As the body's primary means of transportation, legs support the body and enable activities such as walking, running, and dancing. They comprise bones, muscles, and joints that work together to provide stability and strength.

Points of View

1. Tonight, the dance floor will be mine, a stage for the poetry my long legs will write.
2. My legs must push harder, sprint faster, each stride bringing me closer to victory.
3. Pacing the room, I let the rhythm of my steps, the familiar thump of my legs, guide my scattered thoughts toward a plan.
4. A tremor runs through my legs, a silent echo of the fear clawing at me as I face the abyss, but they cannot fail me. Not now.
5. Each step echoes with a complaint from my weary legs, demanding rest. But I need to press on.
6. Fuel your wanderlust! Legs are nature's engineering marvel, a dance of muscles and bone powering your personal rocket boots on life's incredible journey.
7. With a deep breath, I make the leap, trusting in the strength of my legs to carry me across the precarious bridge.
8. The music envelops me, guiding my legs into a dance that is equal parts grace and exuberance.
9. As I approach him, my knees go weak. "Stay strong," I whisper, urging my trembling legs forward.
10. My heart pounding, I run, legs turning into blur beneath me, driving me toward my goal.
11. "I-I just," my voice falters, legs shaking like a newborn deer in the spotlight of the formidable crowd.
12. I stand firm, legs rooted in confidence as I prepare to deliver my speech to the waiting audience.

Lips

The soft, movable parts at the mouth's opening that serve multiple functions. They enable speaking, expressing emotions, kissing, and tasting, playing a crucial role in how we communicate and experience the world around us.

Points of View

1. I'm biting my lip nervously as I wait for the jury's verdict, trying to hide my anxiety.
2. "I'm whispering sweet nothings into her ear, my lips brushing against her skin gently.
3. I'm struggling to find the right words to convey my emotions. My lips are parched, and my tongue feels heavy with unspoken words.
4. I'm savoring the taste of the decadent chocolate cake, my lips tingling with pleasure.
5. I'm pouting my lips in frustration, unable to express my thoughts clearly.
6. I'm pressing my lips together tightly, holding back tears that threaten to spill over.
7. I'm smiling widely, my lips curving up in pure joy as I receive the good news.
8. I'm licking my lips in anticipation, savoring the delicious aroma of freshly brewed coffee.
9. I pursed my lips in disapproval, holding back my criticism.
10. I'm kissing his lips gently, feeling the warmth and tenderness of their touch.
11. A bold swipe of red lipstick transforms my lips. The vibrant color blossoms with each stroke, and confidence washes over me—a surge of power fueled by this simple act.
12. I'm mumbling under my breath, my lips barely moving as I curse my misfortune.

Liver

The liver is a vital organ in the upper right of the abdomen. It detoxifies harmful substances, aids digestion by producing bile, regulates blood sugar and cholesterol levels, synthesizes proteins, and contributes to blood clotting.

Points of View

1. James rubbed his temples, feeling the relentless wave of exhaustion crash over him. "I'm running on empty," he muttered, his voice barely a whisper. It was as if his liver was a beleaguered soldier, battling against a sea of stress and toxins.
2. "I need to feed my liver, help it wage this war against the toxins," he mumbled, his eyes scanning the menu for allies – leafy greens, antioxidant-rich fruits, lean proteins.
3. A sharp pain lanced through his side, making him wince. He pressed a hand there, feeling the throb of discomfort. "Could my liver be raising a red flag?" he wondered, the dread curling like smoke in his mind.
4. James lifted his glass, swirling the ruby red wine within. "To think that this simple pleasure will journey through my liver," he remarked, a note of awe coloring his voice. The intricate dance between indulgence and health was a marvel to him.
5. "I'm so tired," he confessed to the empty room. His voice echoed back at him, a reminder of his solitary struggle. It felt like his liver was a sluggish machine, clogged with toxins and groaning under the strain.
6. "I'm walking a cleaner path now," he shared, his voice firm with resolve. "No alcohol, no junk food. My liver deserves a break, a chance to regain its strength."
7. In the quiet of his thoughts, he sent a silent note of gratitude to his liver. A thankless soldier on the frontlines of his health, tirelessly fighting to keep him whole.

8. "I've been seeking wisdom, ways to support my liver," he explained. His words were infused with newfound respect for the incredible organ that tirelessly toiled within him.

9. "I've become a steward of my health," he declared, "Every decision, every morsel of food is a conscious choice for my liver's well-being."

10. James' hand absently drifted to his abdomen, a dull ache pulsating beneath his fingertips. "Is this a battle cry from my liver?" he mused, fear and concern intermingling in his thoughts.

11. "Every step I take is a stride toward a healthier environment," he shared, his tone resolute. "My liver shouldn't have to battle both my choices and the world around me."

12. "I've learned to listen, to hear my body's whispers," he assured his doctor. "Every twinge, every discomfort could be a signal from my liver, and I don't intend to ignore it."

Lungs

A pair of spongy organs in the chest responsible for breathing. They take in air, absorb oxygen into the bloodstream, and expel carbon dioxide, a waste product of the body's processes.

Points of View

1. I draw in a deep breath, the cool fresh air rushing into my lungs like a rejuvenating elixir, invigorating every cell in my body.
2. I hack out a cough, my lungs straining and wheezing under the assault of my illness. It feels like I'm trying to draw breath through a narrow straw, every gasp a battle.
3. The salty sea breeze fills my lungs, the invigorating scent of the ocean carrying with it a sense of freedom. It's as if my lungs are expanding with the vastness of the sea itself.
4. Excitement grips me, stealing the breath from my lungs. My heart races, pulsing in time with my quick, shallow breaths, as if trying to keep pace with the thrilling surge of adrenaline.
5. I'm gasping for air, the world spinning as my lungs clench in panic. Each shallow breath is a plea for calm, a desperate bid to regain control.
6. I steadily inhale and exhale, my lungs flexing and contracting in a mindful rhythm. Each breath is an act of resistance, a small victory in my quest for better respiratory health.
7. With bated breath, I wait for the results, my lungs held captive by the suspense. The silence is a vacuum, consuming the air around me, leaving my lungs yearning for release.

8. A sharp pain sears through my chest, sending fear ricocheting through my mind. Is it my lungs? Is it something serious? Each throb is a pulsating question mark, an unknown that scares me more than the pain itself.

9. I let out a long, slow exhale, as if I'm blowing away the cobwebs of tension and stress from my lungs. It feels like I'm deflating a balloon, releasing the pent-up pressure within me.

10. I tune into the rhythm of my breathing, finding solace in the steady rise and fall of my lungs. Each inhale is an invitation to life; each exhale a resignation to peace.

11. As I prepare to speak, I fill my lungs with a deep breath. It's a tangible form of courage, inflating my lungs along with my confidence, giving me the strength to voice my thoughts.

12. I marvel at the miraculous network of my lungs, the life-giving force within me. Each breath is a reminder of the fragility and resilience of life, and the silent strength of my body.

Lymph nodes

Small, bean-shaped secondary organs that are part of the body's immune system. Lymph nodes help filter out harmful substances and pathogens from the lymph fluid circulating throughout the body, aiding in the defense against infections.

Points of View

1. A tender sensation throbs at the side of my neck, my fingertips gingerly pressing against the slight bulge of my swollen lymph nodes. It's a silent alarm bell, signaling my body might be waging a war against an unseen invader.

2. My fingers trace the tender area around my lymph nodes, applying gentle pressure in the hopes of alleviating the discomfort. It's like a silent prayer, wishing for the body's natural drainage system to start flowing smoothly again.

3. A rush of relief floods through me as the doctor's words land: the swollen lymph nodes, those tiny lumps that had sparked so much fear, are benign. It feels as if I've been given a new lease on life.

4. A nagging tenderness radiates from my groin, particularly around the lymph node. My mind races with dark possibilities. It feels as if my body's trying to tell me something important, and I can't help but fear it might not be good news.

5. As the doctor assured me my lymph nodes are not cancerous, I let out a breath I didn't realize I had been holding. It's as if I've been granted a reprieve, a chance to live my life without the looming specter of cancer.

6. The realization that my lymph nodes are swollen in multiple areas sends a chill down my spine. It's a feeling of unease that lingers, a constant reminder of the unknown that lies beneath the skin.

7. I find myself filled with a newfound respect for the unsung heroes within me – my lymph nodes. These tiny guardians tirelessly filter out the harmful substances, protecting me from a world of potential infections.

8. I commit to regular exercise, a balanced diet, and adequate hydration, nurturing my body as it nurtures me. It's a small tribute to the delicate network of my lymph nodes, a way of acknowledging their ceaseless vigilance in keeping me healthy.

9. The persistent throbbing in my lymph nodes is a grim reminder that my body is at war. Each pulse of pain underscores the battle being waged beneath the surface, a struggle to overcome an illness.

10. A sense of euphoria washes over me as I take in the news: my biopsy results are clear, and my lymph nodes are cancer-free. It feels like I've been released from an invisible prison, the weight of worry lifting off my shoulders.

11. I marvel at the intricate network of my lymph nodes, silently at work filtering toxins from my body. It's a testament to the incredible machinery within me, tirelessly working to keep me healthy.

12. The wait for my lymph node biopsy results is a ticking clock, anxiety gnawing away with each passing second. I'm caught between hope and fear, praying for a clean bill of health.

Practice Exercises

Instruction: Use this exercise to deepen your understanding of the lesson after reviewing each body part, such as the Adam's Apple or zygote, or after completing all the body parts in a particular letter set—A, B, or Z.

Task 1: Tagging Dialogues: Identify and list the dialogue tags used in the examples.

Task 2: Tracking Action Beats: Analyze the provided examples and identify action beats.

Task 3: Teasing Out Narrative Styles: Review the examples and distinguish between two narrative styles. Mark instances of deep POV that immerse you in a character's emotions or thoughts with a check mark (✓). Use an asterisk (*) to denote shallow POV instances, which focus primarily on surface-level actions or descriptions.

Task 4: Testing Your Skills with New Examples: Write four new phrases or short paragraphs incorporating an action beat and a dialogue tag. Use deep and shallow POV to explore different aspects of the body part discussed in this section.

Mammary Glands

These milk-producing glands develop in females during puberty. They are responsible for lactation, producing milk in response to pregnancy or nursing.

Points of View

1. Martha grimaced, feeling a sudden rush of milk from her mammary glands. Her body had become a nourishing factory for her baby, a miracle marred slightly by the persistent ache in her breasts.
2. Rachel choked back tears, enduring the painful sting from cracked nipples and the heavy ache from her swollen mammary glands. Breastfeeding felt more like a battlefield than the peaceful act she had imagined.
3. With her infant nestled close, Brea felt an overwhelming love. The act of her baby latching onto her mammary glands stirred wonder within her, solidifying an intimate bond through each feeding session.
4. Martha discreetly adjusted her nursing pads, grateful for their concealment. Despite the continuous dampness from her mammary glands, the growing bond with her baby during feedings made every discomfort worth it.
5. Sarah blushed, looking at her damp blouse, a constant reminder of her overactive mammary glands. She was slowly realizing the surprising physical demands of motherhood.
6. Alex sighed, appreciating the nursery's solitude. Even though breastfeeding sometimes felt isolating, the quiet moments bonding with her baby through her nourishing mammary glands were gratifying.

7. Jessica watched her baby latch with an anxious gaze. A fear constantly lingered – were her mammary glands producing enough milk for her baby? The question was a frequent uninvited guest in her mind.

8. Marah yawned, feeling drained by the relentless cycle of breastfeeding. Her mammary glands worked tirelessly, leaving her feeling like she was being consumed by the process.

9. As Marah held her nursing baby, her eyes welled up with tears. Every feeding, every drop of milk her mammary glands produced, fortified their bond, enveloping her in a love she hadn't known before.

10. With careful hands, Jessica massaged her aching breasts, amazed by the capability of her own mammary glands. Despite the discomfort, she felt a sense of awe at the abundance of milk she was producing.

11. Heart pounding, Brea adjusted her nursing cover in public, a wave of vulnerability sweeping over her. Yet, her instinct to nourish her child, driven by her mammary glands, outweighed her fear, giving her strength.

12. Grinning, Alex thought of her normal bras, waiting for their turn once her breastfeeding journey ended. Despite the challenges faced by her mammary glands, looking at her baby, she knew without doubt, it was all worth it.

Mesentery

A double layer of tissue in the abdomen that acts like a supporting hammock for the intestines. It secures these organs to the back wall of the abdomen. This essential structure contains critical pathways, including blood vessels, nerves, and lymphatic channels, all working together to keep the intestines functioning properly.

Points of View

1. Art doubled over, a jolt of searing pain ripping through his abdomen. He clutched his belly, gasping for breath. It felt like his insides were being squeezed in a vice. The pain came in waves, intensifying after every meal, and his mesentery contracting violently like a vice tightening around his gut.

2. Adam grimaced, hand splayed over his belly. "It's like something in my mesentery pulled," he managed between breaths.

3. Hunched over in pain, Missy held her abdomen. "Feels like needles stabbing through my mesentery."

4. Sarah fiddled with the button of her pants, her distended abdomen pulsating with discomfort. "I swear, even my mesentery feels bloated."

5. As John hoisted a heavy box, a sudden fear seized him. "Could straining like this cause a hernia in the mesentery?"

6. Elizabeth crossed her legs, restlessness flitting across her face. "Feels like my bladder's pushing against my mesentery. I need the restroom again."

7. With a frown creasing his forehead, Mike gingerly rubbed his belly. "Feels like my mesentery's acting up. So many digestive issues."

8. Lizzy scanned the room for non-dairy options, a worried crease on her brow. My mesentery is having trouble processing certain foods.

9. Kam gripped her stomach, her face pale. "My mesentery feels twisted. I'm so nauseous and dizzy."
10. Timothy took a slow sip of his antacid, the burning sensation in his gut unrelenting. "My mesentery feels on fire with this acid reflux," he said.
11. The online articles about intestinal blockages wouldn't leave Sophia's mind. Every ache and gurgle felt amplified, and she couldn't shake the image of her mesentery all twisted up.
12. David's gaze lingered on the illustration of the digestive system, particularly the intricate network of the mesentery. Could that be the culprit behind the persistent inflammation in his abdomen?

Practice Exercises

Instruction: Use this exercise to deepen your understanding of the lesson after reviewing each body part, such as the Adam's Apple or zygote, or after completing all the body parts in a particular letter set—A, B, or Z.

Task 1: Tagging Dialogues: Identify and list the dialogue tags used in the examples.

Task 2: Tracking Action Beats: Analyze the provided examples and identify action beats.

Task 3: Teasing Out Narrative Styles: Review the examples and distinguish between two narrative styles. Mark instances of deep POV that immerse you in a character's emotions or thoughts with a check mark (✓). Use an asterisk (*) to denote shallow POV instances, which focus primarily on surface-level actions or descriptions.

Task 4: Testing Your Skills with New Examples: Write four new phrases or short paragraphs incorporating an action beat and a dialogue tag. Use deep and shallow POV to explore different aspects of the body part discussed in this section.

Mind

The component of a person that processes thoughts, feelings, and awareness of the world. It handles our memories, perceptions, and decision-making, crucial for navigating and interacting with our surroundings and inner experiences.

Points of View

1. His mind was a whirlwind, thoughts tangling and emotions spiraling. He paced the room, hands in his hair, unable to rest.
2. With a confident smile, she solved the puzzle in seconds, her sharp mind racing ahead of everyone else in the room. "Try something harder next time," she challenged.
3. "I can't get you out of my mind," he confessed, eyes locked on hers, voice trembling with intensity.
4. She tapped her temple, brows furrowed, mind working overtime. "There has to be a solution here somewhere," she mumbled.
5. The memory overtook her mind suddenly, and she was back on that rainy day, tears in her eyes and his laughter in her ears.
6. His mind was like a steel trap, unyielding and unforgiving. He recited the details flawlessly, not missing a beat.
7. "I've changed my mind," she announced voice firm, eyes bright with determination. She crossed her arms, resolute.
8. His fists clenched, and his mind was in turmoil, torn between what he knew was right and what he felt in his heart.
9. The melody played in her mind, a sweet, lingering reminder of their first dance. She closed her eyes, swaying to the rhythm only she could hear.
10. Decision made, her mind clear and focused, she picked up the phone to accept the job offer.

11. "I can't make up my mind," he admitted, rubbing his forehead in frustration, eyes darting between the two choices before him.
12. Her mind raced, thoughts scattered and disordered. She sighed, raking a hand through her hair, feeling more lost than ever.

Note: In creative writing, the "mind" is more than a physical aspect of the body; it's a complex landscape for exploring a character's thoughts, emotions, and motivations. Utilizing the mind as a literary device allows for a deeper connection to characters and can reveal hidden layers of their personality, driving both character development and plot progression.

Mouth

An opening in the face that serves multiple functions. It is the entry point for food and drinks, facilitating the beginning of digestion. The mouth also acts as the exit point for sound and speech.

Points of View

1. His mouth tasted like ash, a stark reminder of the fire he'd narrowly escaped.
2. Sarah's mouth curved into a smile as she heard the good news.
3. "I can't believe you're here," he whispered, mouth agape in surprise.
4. Licking her dry lips, she forced her mouth to form an apology.
5. The sweetness of the ice cream brought a shiver of delight as it hit her mouth.
6. His mouth hardened into a firm line as he made the difficult decision.
7. "This pizza is amazing," she declared, her mouth full.
8. His mouth twitched with amusement as he watched the playful puppy.
9. Bitter regret filled her mouth as she confessed her secret.
10. Her mouth moved in silent prayer, seeking divine intervention.
11. "I have to go," he muttered, mouth set in a grim line.
12. A gasp escaped her mouth as the car swerved.

Muscles

Tissues in the body made up of specialized cells that contract or relax to produce movement. These actions range from everyday activities like walking and talking to more complex actions in sports and exercises.

Points of View

1. Alex rubbed his temples, muscles knotting with tension as the exam approached. "I hope I'm ready for this," he muttered, flipping through his notes.
2. She stumbled at the top of the hill, muscles aching from the climb, and gasped for air.
3. He lifted the heavy weights, his muscles rippling, and a confident smile playing on his lips.
4. "I need to stretch," she sighed, bending down, her muscles protesting.
5. He flexed his arm, muscles straining under the weight, then relaxed, satisfied.
6. He froze, fear coiling in his muscles, eyes darting to every shadow.
7. Mrs. O'Problem sank into the hot bath, muscles relaxing instantly and a contented sigh escaping her lips.
8. "I'm so tired," he grumbled, muscles slackening, as he collapsed on the sofa.
9. The wind picked up, and she shivered, feeling it run through her muscles. She hugged herself tighter, looking around.
10. His muscles twitched, and he bounced on the balls of his feet, ready for the race. "Just a few more minutes," he muttered to himself.
11. He wiped his forehead, feeling sweat trickle down his muscles as he worked out. "Just one more set," he panted.
12. Fifi hefted the box, wincing as her muscles strained. "It's heavier than it looks," she told Jim, setting it down with a thud.

Myometrium

The myometrium is the middle layer of the uterine wall, composed of smooth muscle cells and connective tissue. It contracts during childbirth to expel the baby from the uterus.

Points of View

1. She placed her hand over her abdomen, marveling at her myometrium's strength and resilience during childbirth.
2. The myometrium, a powerful layer of muscle and tissue, stood ready for the marathon of birth.
3. "The contractions you're feeling are your myometrium at work," the midwife informed, monitoring the contraction pattern.
4. She clutched her belly, the contractions of her myometrium demanding her full attention.
5. Her myometrium, a hidden powerhouse, flexed and released in rhythm with her breathing.
6. The myometrium was a silent player in the game of birth, flexing and relaxing without fanfare.
7. "Your myometrium contracts to push the baby out," the doctor explained, demonstrating with his hands.
8. She massaged her abdomen, wondering if she could soothe her contracting myometrium.
9. Pain radiated from her lower abdomen, her myometrium performing its duty with unwavering commitment.
10. The myometrium's role in childbirth was a testament to the body's amazing capability.
11. "During labor, the myometrium thins out to allow the baby to pass through," the nurse explained.
12. He studied the anatomy diagram, trying to understand the role of the myometrium in childbirth.

Practice Exercises

Instruction: Use this exercise to deepen your understanding of the lesson after reviewing each body part, such as the Adam's Apple or zygote, or after completing all the body parts in a particular letter set—A, B, or Z.

Task 1: Tagging Dialogues: Identify and list the dialogue tags used in the examples.

Task 2: Tracking Action Beats: Analyze the provided examples and identify action beats.

Task 3: Teasing Out Narrative Styles: Review the examples and distinguish between two narrative styles. Mark instances of deep POV that immerse you in a character's emotions or thoughts with a check mark (✓). Use an asterisk (*) to denote shallow POV instances, which focus primarily on surface-level actions or descriptions.

Task 4: Testing Your Skills with New Examples: Write four new phrases or short paragraphs incorporating an action beat and a dialogue tag. Use deep and shallow POV to explore different aspects of the body part discussed in this section.

Neck

The part of the body that connects the head to the torso. The neck contains blood vessels, nerves, and muscles that support head movement and enable communication between the brain and other body parts.

Points of View

1. As I step into the haunted house, shadows lurk in every corner, and a chilling shiver travels down my neck.
2. He wrapped a scarf around his neck, the cold wind biting his skin.
3. "This tie is a bit tight," he complained, tugging at the fabric around his neck.
4. I tilt my neck, squinting at the abstract painting, trying to grasp its hidden meaning.
5. Panic surges within me, sweat trickling down my neck, each drop echoing my fear.
6. Her neck gleamed with a delicate silver chain, a subtle accent to her elegance.
7. "I think I pulled something," she winced, fingers kneading the tense muscles in her neck.
8. Straining to see over the crowd, I crane my neck, the distant stage barely visible.
9. Embarrassment floods my face, and a sudden heat rushes to my neck as his eyes turn my way.
10. He leaned in, his lips brushing her neck, eliciting a soft giggle from her.
11. "I need a pillow," I sigh, the stiffness in my neck a nagging reminder of hours spent studying.
12. She wore her hair up, the elegant curve of the nape of her neck on full display.

Nose

Located in the middle of the face, the nose is used for smelling and breathing. It features two openings, known as nostrils, through which air is inhaled and exhaled.

Points of View

1. The warm, comforting scent of fresh-baked cookies fills my nose, instantly taking me back to my grandmother's cozy kitchen.
2. Her nose crinkles adorably as she bursts into laughter, eyes sparkling joyfully.
3. "I can smell the rain," I murmured, lifting my nose toward the sky, feeling the subtle change in the air.
4. He pinches his nose, his face contorting as he tries to escape the foul odor.
5. A sudden tickle in my nose builds, warning me of an imminent sneeze, and I scramble for a tissue.
6. His nose is buried in a thick book, the world around him forgotten as he loses himself in the story.
7. "Something's burning," I say, my nose wrinkling in distaste as the acrid smell permeates the room.
8. She rubs her nose vigorously, her face flushed from the biting cold.
9. As the calming scent of roses fills my nose, I feel my anxiety melt away, replaced by serene tranquility.
10. He winced in pain, recalling how he broke his nose in a rough football game.
11. "Your perfume is strong," I comment, my nose twitching, the fragrance almost overwhelming.
12. She subtly brushes her nose with her sleeve, hoping no one notices the gesture.

Nostrils

The two external openings of the nose. Nostrils allow air to enter and exit for breathing and smelling. They also filter and warm the air before it reaches the lungs.

Points of View

1. The crisp, fresh smell of pine hits my nostrils, and I'm immediately transported back to cozy Christmas mornings.
2. "I can't breathe," I wheeze, feeling my nostrils flare with each desperate effort to draw in air.
3. A rush of cold air fills my nostrils, invigorating me, snapping me to attention.
4. The rich smell of the sea fills my nostrils, soothing my mind and bringing a rare sense of peace.
5. "Do you smell that?" I ask, my nostrils twitching, trying to identify the unfamiliar scent.
6. "This smells amazing," she exclaims, her nostrils dilating as she inhales the delicious aroma from the dish before her.
7. Her nostrils flare, and her eyes narrow, the anger in her face unmistakable.
8. She sniffs, nostrils quivering with delight as she steps into the fragrant garden, flowers blooming all around her.
9. Smoke curls into her nostrils, causing her to cough and wave her hand in front of her face.
10. She pinches her nostrils, grimacing to block out the unpleasant smell.
11. His nostrils flare, and his breath comes out in an annoyed huff, his frustration evident.
12. Her nostrils flare ever so slightly, her eyes lighting up as they catch the scent of her favorite perfume.

Practice Exercises

Instruction: Use this exercise to deepen your understanding of the lesson after reviewing each body part, such as the Adam's Apple or zygote, or after completing all the body parts in a particular letter set—A, B, or Z.

Task 1: Tagging Dialogues: Identify and list the dialogue tags used in the examples.

Task 2: Tracking Action Beats: Analyze the provided examples and identify action beats.

Task 3: Teasing Out Narrative Styles: Review the examples and distinguish between two narrative styles. Mark instances of deep POV that immerse you in a character's emotions or thoughts with a check mark (✓). Use an asterisk (*) to denote shallow POV instances, which focus primarily on surface-level actions or descriptions.

Task 4: Testing Your Skills with New Examples: Write four new phrases or short paragraphs incorporating an action beat and a dialogue tag. Use deep and shallow POV to explore different aspects of the body part discussed in this section.

Ovaries

The female reproductive organs that produce eggs (ova) and certain hormones. The two ovaries are in the lower abdomen on both sides of the uterus.

Points of View

1. She closed her eyes, willing the ache in her ovaries to disappear. Each deep breath seemed to aggravate the dull throb. Her hand instinctively rested on her stomach, pressing down ever so slightly on the area where her ovaries were. "Maybe some deep breaths will help the pain in my ovaries," she muttered to herself.

2. A sharp pain in her ovaries reminded her that her period was due.

3. Her ovaries were affected by polycystic ovary syndrome, a condition she had to manage daily.

4. She winced, the discomfort in her ovaries signaling the onset of ovulation.

5. A jolt of searing pain ripped through my abdomen, doubling me over. Memories flooded back - the frantic rush to the hospital, the doctor's grim diagnosis: a ruptured ovarian cyst. I squeezed my eyes shut, willing the phantom ache in my ovaries to subside.

6. The ultrasound image of her ovaries was strange and foreign, yet fascinating.

7. "I'm considering freezing my eggs," she mentioned, contemplating the future of her ovaries.

8. The fertility medication made her ovaries ache, a reminder of her longing for a child.

9. The word "cancer" hung heavy in the air, shattering the normalcy of my life. My diagnosis of ovarian cancer had been a brutal awakening, forcing me to confront my own mortality. Everything I had taken for granted - my health and future - was suddenly questioned. My thoughts fixated on my ovaries, the source of the disease that had upended my life.

10. Her ovaries were healthy, according to her latest check-up.

11. She put a hot water bottle on her lower abdomen, hoping to soothe her aching ovaries.

12. "I might have ovarian cysts," she admitted, her voice barely a whisper. Her hand fluttered down to her stomach, rubbing it nervously. A grimace flickered across her face, a silent reflection of the worry gnawing at her about the possible return of cysts in her ovaries.

Oviduct

Also known as the fallopian tube, it is one of two tubes that transport the egg from the ovary to the uterus each month in females. Fertilization usually occurs in the oviduct.

Points of View

1. She could almost feel the tiny movement in her oviduct, the hopeful journey of life.
2. The oviduct was her silent path to motherhood, the gateway to a new life.
3. "The blockage is in your oviduct," the doctor explained, pointing at the scan.
4. She held her lower abdomen, contemplating the intricate workings of her oviduct.
5. The pain shot through her oviduct like a lightning bolt, leaving her breathless.
6. Her oviducts were silent conduits of life, paths seldom acknowledged.
7. "We'll need to check your oviducts," the gynecologist advised, a note of concern in her voice.
8. She winced, feeling an odd twinge in the area where she imagined her oviduct to be.
9. Each month her oviducts carried precious potential, a symphony of hope and anticipation.
10. His medical studies introduced him to the marvel that was the oviduct.
11. "The fertilization usually happens in the oviduct," the biology teacher explained to the class.
12. He studied the textbook diagram, trying to understand the journey of an egg through the oviduct.

Practice Exercises

Instruction: Use this exercise to deepen your understanding of the lesson after reviewing each body part, such as the Adam's Apple or zygote, or after completing all the body parts in a particular letter set—A, B, or Z.

Task 1: Tagging Dialogues: Identify and list the dialogue tags used in the examples.

Task 2: Tracking Action Beats: Analyze the provided examples and identify action beats.

Task 3: Teasing Out Narrative Styles: Review the examples and distinguish between two narrative styles. Mark instances of deep POV that immerse you in a character's emotions or thoughts with a check mark (✓). Use an asterisk (*) to denote shallow POV instances, which focus primarily on surface-level actions or descriptions.

Task 4: Testing Your Skills with New Examples: Write four new phrases or short paragraphs incorporating an action beat and a dialogue tag. Use deep and shallow POV to explore different aspects of the body part discussed in this section.

Pancreas

A long, tadpole-shaped gland located in the upper abdomen behind and extending to the left of the stomach. It plays a vital role in digestion by releasing enzymes that break down food and in hormone production, including insulin.

Points of View

1. She could almost feel the surge of insulin her pancreas released at the first bite of her sugary snack.
2. The pancreas, ever vigilant, prepared to break down the onslaught of food.
3. "I'm afraid your pancreas isn't producing enough insulin," the doctor said with a somber tone.
4. She held her abdomen, silently thanking her pancreas for its hard work after a big meal.
5. He imagined his pancreas, quietly producing enzymes to aid in digestion.
6. The pancreas is the unsung hero in the daily battle of digestion.
7. "My pancreas just can't handle this diet," she complained to her friend over a plate of greasy food.
8. He traced the area over his pancreas, imagining the delicate balance of hormones within.
9. She could practically feel her pancreas working overtime to deal with her sudden sugar binge.
10. Even amid chaos, the pancreas worked diligently, producing just the right amount of digestive enzymes.
11. "My pancreas isn't as efficient as it used to be," he admitted, avoiding the dessert menu.
12. She took a deep breath, visualizing her pancreas, the essential organ she so often took for granted.

Parathyroid Glands

These are tiny glands in the neck that produce parathyroid hormone, which regulates calcium levels in the body.

Points of View

1. The sudden weakness in her bones made her wonder if her parathyroid glands were keeping her calcium levels balanced.
2. The parathyroid glands, small but mighty, maintained the delicate balance of calcium in the body.
3. "The parathyroid glands regulate calcium, an essential mineral for bone health," the physician explained.
4. He tapped his fingers against his neck, wondering if his parathyroid glands were doing their job.
5. Her aching muscles made her question if her parathyroid glands were functioning optimally.
6. The parathyroid glands, nestled in the neck, played an essential role in bone and muscle health.
7. "I think there might be an issue with my parathyroid glands," she confessed to her doctor.
8. She gently massaged her neck, hoping to stimulate her parathyroid glands into action.
9. He thought of his parathyroid glands, responsible for keeping his calcium levels in check.
10. The parathyroid glands silently work to keep the body's minerals in harmony.
11. "Your parathyroid glands are crucial for maintaining the balance of calcium in your body," the endocrinologist emphasized.
12. He swallowed hard, mindful of the essential work his parathyroid glands performed behind the scenes.

Pelvis

An extensive bony framework near the base of the spine in humans and many vertebrates. It connects the spine to the legs and supports several organs in the lower abdomen. The pelvis is also a term used to describe the top area of the tube that carries urine from the kidney to the bladder.

Points of View

1. The dancer's graceful movement began in her pelvis.
2. As I stretched, a refreshing tension enveloped the muscles surrounding my pelvis, releasing the day's stress, and connecting me with my body in a moment of mindfulness.
3. Hours of relentless sitting took their toll, a constant, dull ache in my pelvis nagging at me. It was more than mere discomfort; it was a draining, a constant reminder of the long day's work.
4. He hit the ground hard, a jarring sensation in his pelvis.
5. Sage's pelvis tilted and shifted as the horse beneath her moved.
6. My pelvis pivoted, a subtle but crucial movement, and my arm followed in a fluid, practiced motion. The football soared with precision, a culmination of years of training and instinct. I watched it cut through the air, knowing it was a perfect throw.
7. My physiotherapist's eyes twinkled, and a warm smile spread across his face. "The pelvis," he said, leaning in as if sharing a profound secret, "is vital for our body's support." His words resonated with me, a simple truth linking anatomy, function, and how we move.
8. "The human pelvis is impressive," the teacher exclaimed.

9. An agonizing ache flared in my pelvis, and my hand instinctively went to my side, gently cradling the injured area. Memories of the accident flooded back, mixed with frustration and a newfound vulnerability.
10. "Your pelvis is fractured," the doctor said with a concerned look.
11. She touched her hips, feeling the firm structure of her pelvis.
12. A sharp pain in Rylan's pelvis reminded him of his painful fall.

Penis

The male reproductive organ that also lets urine out of the body. It has an extended part called the shaft and a tip called the glans. The penis can become firm when filled with blood, which is vital in sexual activity.

Points of View

1. A wave of embarrassment washed over him as he thought about discussing his penis's health with the doctor.
2. The penis, a critical component of both the urinary and reproductive systems, frequently encounters its own set of challenges.
3. "Men need to pay more attention to their penis health," the doctor said sternly.
4. He glanced down, worried about the unusual symptom affecting his penis.
5. A pang of concern settled in his mind, his penis not behaving normally.
6. The penis plays an essential role in human reproduction.
7. "Your penis health can indicate overall health issues," the nurse pointed out.
8. He zipped up his jeans carefully, mindful of his penis.
9. He was nervous about the physical exam, particularly the inspection of his penis.
10. The penis is often a source of anxiety for many men.
11. "It's important to check your penis regularly for any changes," the doctor advised.
12. He adjusted himself in his pants, trying to find a comfortable position for his penis.

Peritoneum

A thin, transparent membrane that lines the abdominal cavity and covers the abdominal organs, providing a protective layer.

Points of View

1. Her hands rested on her abdomen, a dull ache radiating from beneath her peritoneum.
2. Surgeons had to navigate through the peritoneum to reach the afflicted organs.
3. "Your peritoneum is inflamed," the doctor said, showing her the scan results.
4. He winced, the pain in his abdomen making him hyperaware of his peritoneum.
5. A sharp pain seared through her peritoneum, taking her breath away.
6. Infections in the peritoneum can lead to severe complications.
7. "We may need to operate to remove the adhesions from your peritoneum," the surgeon said.
8. She doubled over, the pain under her peritoneum sharp and sudden.
9. His breath hitched as a searing pain radiated from his peritoneum.
10. The peritoneum plays a crucial role in the body's defense against infection.
11. My heart hammered in my chest. This was it. The nephrologist was laying out the path ahead. "Peritoneal dialysis," he said calmly and measuredly, "might be the most suitable option for you." The word 'peritoneum' hung in the air momentarily, a new term I'd have to learn alongside this new reality.
12. He leaned back in the chair, trying to ease the discomfort around his peritoneum.

Pineal Gland

A tiny, pinecone-shaped gland in the brain that produces melatonin, a hormone that regulates the sleep-wake cycle. It functions like a natural nightlight or seasonal clock, guiding the body's internal rhythms.

Points of View

1. Her sleeplessness was driving her to despair; she wondered if her pineal gland was malfunctioning.
2. The pineal gland, often overlooked, plays a crucial role in our sleep-wake cycles.
3. "Your pineal gland could be responsible for your sleep issues," the doctor suggested.
4. She yawned, the exhaustion seeping into her bones, her pineal gland working overtime.
5. Despite his exhaustion, sleep eluded him, as if his pineal gland were on strike.
6. The pineal gland controls the production of melatonin, influencing our sleep patterns.
7. "The pineal gland is crucial for maintaining our circadian rhythm," the neurologist explained.
8. He tossed and turned, his sleep disrupted, as if his pineal gland had forgotten its role.
9. She blinked against the harsh light, wondering if it was messing with her pineal gland.
10. The pineal gland, though small, carries significant influence over our well-being.
11. "Exposure to light at night can disrupt your pineal gland's functions," the sleep therapist warned.
12. He sat in the dark room, hoping to trigger his pineal gland into releasing sleep-inducing melatonin.

Pituitary Gland

Often called the "master gland," this pea-sized powerhouse is located at the base of the brain. It plays a central role in managing body functions by producing and releasing a variety of hormones. These hormones regulate growth, stress responses, reproductive processes, milk production, water balance in the body, and even emotional bonding.

Points of View

1. The unrelenting severity of her migraines served as a constant reminder of the trouble in her pituitary gland.
2. The pituitary gland regulates the function of most other endocrine glands, hence its "master gland" nickname.
3. "Your pituitary gland is functioning normally," the doctor confirmed, putting her at ease.
4. He rubbed his temples, the pain indicative of pressure on his pituitary gland.
5. Her pituitary gland wasn't playing fair, wreaking havoc on her hormone levels.
6. Despite its small size, the pituitary gland has a vital role in hormone regulation.
7. "The pituitary gland controls your growth hormone," explained the endocrinologist.
8. He sighed, his pituitary gland's malfunction leading to countless medical issues.
9. Her body felt out of sync, as if her pituitary gland was orchestrating a symphony of chaos.
10. Disorders of the pituitary gland can impact overall health significantly.
11. "We'll need to monitor your pituitary gland regularly," the doctor advised.
12. She swallowed the prescribed medication, hoping it would normalize her pituitary gland's function.

Prostate Gland

A small, walnut-sized gland in men that surrounds the neck of the bladder and urethra. It produces a fluid that nourishes and transports sperm.

Points of View

1. His prostate gland's troubles were an unwelcome reminder of advancing age.
2. The prostate gland plays a crucial role in male reproductive health.
3. "Your prostate gland is slightly enlarged," the doctor informed him, sparking concern.
4. He grappled with the discomfort, his prostate gland causing more trouble than usual.
5. Regular check-ups are essential for early detection of prostate gland issues.
6. He winced, his prostate gland making itself known through persistent discomfort.
7. Prostate gland health is a significant concern for men, especially as they age.
8. He adjusted his position, trying to find a comfortable spot, his prostate gland causing a dull ache.
9. Dread coiled in his gut as the doctor spoke of a possible malignancy in his prostate gland.
10. "We need to do a prostate-specific antigen (PSA) test," the doctor suggested, explaining the next steps. This test helps assess the health of your prostate gland.
11. A chill ran down his spine at the thought of surgery on his prostate glands.
12. "The surgery was successful. We were able to remove the entire tumor in your prostate gland," the surgeon reassured him.

Pupils

The pupils are the black circular openings in the center of the eyes. They control the amount of light that enters. They dilate (expand) in low-light conditions and constrict (shrink) in bright light.

Points of View

1. Her pupils dilated, drinking in the scant light as she navigated the dimly-lit room.
2. The pupils react to light conditions, a feature vital for vision.
3. "Your pupils are dilating normally," the optometrist reported, flashing a small light into her eyes.
4. His pupils constricted, squinting in the harsh midday sun.
5. Fear sparked in her chest as she noticed the unequal size of his pupils, an ominous sign.
6. Certain drugs and medications can cause pupil dilation or constriction.
7. "Her pupils aren't responding to light," the nurse murmured, concern creasing her brow.
8. He blinked, his pupils adjusting to the sudden flood of brightness as the curtains were drawn.
9. Her pupils expanded, soaking in the beauty of the night sky, stars sprinkling the inky canvas.
10. A flashlight is often used to check the responsiveness of pupils during a physical exam.
11. "You may experience temporary blurred vision or light sensitivity due to dilated pupils," the doctor warned after the eye examination.
12. He stared at his reflection, watching his pupils dilate and constrict as he flicked the bathroom light on and off.

Practice Exercises

Instruction: Use this exercise to deepen your understanding of the lesson after reviewing each body part, such as the Adam's Apple or zygote, or after completing all the body parts in a particular letter set—A, B, or Z.

Task 1: Tagging Dialogues: Identify and list the dialogue tags used in the examples.

Task 2: Tracking Action Beats: Analyze the provided examples and identify action beats.

Task 3: Teasing Out Narrative Styles: Review the examples and distinguish between two narrative styles. Mark instances of deep POV that immerse you in a character's emotions or thoughts with a check mark (✓). Use an asterisk (*) to denote shallow POV instances, which focus primarily on surface-level actions or descriptions.

Task 4: Testing Your Skills with New Examples: Write four new phrases or short paragraphs incorporating an action beat and a dialogue tag. Use deep and shallow POV to explore different aspects of the body part discussed in this section.

Quadriceps

Often shortened to "quads," are a group of four large muscles at the front of the thigh. These muscles work together to help straighten the leg at the knee and are crucial for walking, running, and jumping.

Points of View

1. Rylan winced, feeling the burn in his quadriceps as he pedaled harder. This hill was a beast, but he was determined to conquer it.
2. Marah observed the cyclist's quadriceps flexing and relaxing rhythmically. She knew from her own experience that this climb was brutal.
3. Jessica flexed her legs, feeling her quadriceps harden with the effort. She could kick high, and her target was within reach.
4. Rylan collapsed onto the park bench, his quadriceps screaming in protest. He'd pushed too hard today, he admitted to himself.
5. Marah watched as the ballet dancer leaped gracefully, his quadriceps working hard to propel him into the air.
6. The coach reminded his team to "remember to stretch your quadriceps. We don't want any pulled muscles."
7. Marah bent her knees and then launched into a sprint, her quadriceps powering her forward.
8. James felt the familiar pull in his quadriceps, reminding him that his gym routine had been too leg-heavy yesterday.
9. Jessica watched her personal trainer, noting how the defined quadriceps on his legs strained as he demonstrated the squat technique.
10. She jumped and landed smoothly, her quadriceps absorbing the impact with practiced ease.
11. "I need to work on strengthening my quadriceps," Rylan told his fitness instructor, grimacing as he attempted a lunge.
12. "Look at the definition in his quadriceps!" James commented, his gaze locked onto the runner sprinting past them.

Practice Exercises

Instruction: Use this exercise to deepen your understanding of the lesson after reviewing each body part, such as the Adam's Apple or zygote, or after completing all the body parts in a particular letter set—A, B, or Z.

Task 1: Tagging Dialogues: Identify and list the dialogue tags used in the examples.

Task 2: Tracking Action Beats: Analyze the provided examples and identify action beats.

Task 3: Teasing Out Narrative Styles: Review the examples and distinguish between two narrative styles. Mark instances of deep POV that immerse you in a character's emotions or thoughts with a check mark (✓). Use an asterisk (*) to denote shallow POV instances, which focus primarily on surface-level actions or descriptions.

Task 4: Testing Your Skills with New Examples: Write four new phrases or short paragraphs incorporating an action beat and a dialogue tag. Use deep and shallow POV to explore different aspects of the body part discussed in this section.

Rectum

The final segment of the large intestine that connects to the anus. It stores fecal matter until it's expelled from the body.

Points of View

1. Marah, ever the gossip, leaned in conspiratorially. "Did you hear? Shaquille has a perfect rectum!" Shaquille blushed furiously, muttering, "rectum? No, Marah, perfect record!"
2. "Ugh, Sage," grumbled Sage, interpreting the surprisingly deep protests from his rectum. "Those burritos were a bad idea. We both know it."
3. Trapped in rush hour traffic, Tim felt his patience wearing thin. It was becoming as fragile as a rectum thermometer.
4. Fifi shuffled uncomfortably. Time for a visit to the "back passage express," she grumbled, wary of the pending rectum relief.
5. Shaquille's rumbling rectum roared, a rhythmic reminder of the chili disaster he'd bravely (or foolishly) consumed.
6. A peculiar tingling sensation danced across his nether regions. Had he sat on something strange, or was this a new message from his disgruntled rectum?
7. Feeling the pressure build, Alex envisioned himself as Sisyphus, forever condemned to roll the boulder—or, in his case, a certain type of sausage—up the hill of his rectum.
8. The habanero salsa declared war on Josh's digestive system. His rectum, a valiant but ultimately doomed fortress, braced for the fiery onslaught.
9. Shaquille recalled the health class in school, learning about the rectum—the final station before the body expels waste.
10. Torn between pride and practicality, Brea debated whether to admit defeat and excuse herself or soldier through the increasingly urgent demands of her rectum during the critical presentation.

11. Dr. Reginald Bottom proudly unveiled his latest invention: the Rectal-o-Meter, a revolutionary device for measuring rectum fortitude. A collective eye roll rippled through the medical conference.

12. Sweat beaded on Alex's brow as the clock ticked down to his big audition. Would his carefully crafted lines flow flawlessly, or would a sudden, traitorous rebellion from his rectum derail his entire performance?

Ribs

Ribs are long, curved bones that form a cage around the chest (thoracic) cavity, protecting the heart, lungs, and other internal organs. Their primary function is to aid respiration.

Points of View

1. Sage hugged herself, the chill penetrating her coat and making her ribs ache with cold.
2. A dull pain throbbed in Alex's ribs, the memory of the soccer game injury flaring up.
3. "Watch your ribs," the coach called out, as the football player took a risky tackle.
4. She held her side, wincing in pain. "I think I might have bruised my ribs."
5. Sage laughed so hard, her ribs aching with the exertion, pure joy echoing through her.
6. Shaquille's ribs pressed painfully against the cold ground, the fall from the bike more severe than he had initially thought.
7. He laid his hand on his ribs, grimacing. "That punch was harder than I thought."
8. The doctor pointed at the X-ray. "See these shadows? They're on your ribs."
9. Marah could feel her heart pounding against her ribs, the anxiety of the situation escalating.
10. After a long day, Alex stretched, his tired muscles protesting, his ribs expanding with the deep, fulfilling breath.
11. "Can you feel this?" the doctor asked, her hand gently pressing on his lower ribs.
12. "You could count his ribs," she murmured, horrified at the extent of the starvation.

Practice Exercises

Instruction: Use this exercise to deepen your understanding of the lesson after reviewing each body part, such as the Adam's Apple or zygote, or after completing all the body parts in a particular letter set—A, B, or Z.

Task 1: Tagging Dialogues: Identify and list the dialogue tags used in the examples.

Task 2: Tracking Action Beats: Analyze the provided examples and identify action beats.

Task 3: Teasing Out Narrative Styles: Review the examples and distinguish between two narrative styles. Mark instances of deep POV that immerse you in a character's emotions or thoughts with a check mark (✓). Use an asterisk (*) to denote shallow POV instances, which focus primarily on surface-level actions or descriptions.

Task 4: Testing Your Skills with New Examples: Write four new phrases or short paragraphs incorporating an action beat and a dialogue tag. Use deep and shallow POV to explore different aspects of the body part discussed in this section.

Salivary Glands

Small glands in the mouth that produce saliva. This liquid helps moisten food, breaks down starches, and facilitates swallowing. The three main types are called parotid, submandibular, and sublingual glands.

Points of View

1. A spicy sensation tingled her tongue, prompting her salivary glands into overdrive.
2. His mouth was as dry as a desert, his salivary glands seemingly on strike.
3. Anticipation had her salivary glands working overtime; the aroma of the home-cooked meal was irresistible.
4. The hot spice ignited her taste buds, setting her salivary glands into a frenzy.
5. "See, when you chew, your salivary glands produce saliva that starts breaking down the food," she explained to her son.
6. His salivary glands reacted instantly to the tartness of the lemon, a sour shockwave coursing through his mouth.
7. A metallic taste filled her mouth, her salivary glands working to cleanse the foreign sensation.
8. "The dryness of your mouth may be due to blocked salivary glands," the doctor said, his tone clinical.
9. His salivary glands kicked into high gear as the savory scent of the barbecue wafted over him.
10. The sugar on her tongue sent an immediate signal to her salivary glands, drowning her mouth in saliva.
11. Despite the dehydration, his salivary glands tried to lubricate his parched mouth.
12. Her mouth watered uncontrollably, her salivary glands reacting to the mouthwatering dish.

Scalp

This is the skin covering the head, excluding the face. It houses hair follicles, sweat and oil glands, and nerves and blood vessels.

Points of View

1. A tickling sensation danced across her scalp as the stylist ran her fingers through her hair.
2. He scratched his scalp, the stubble of his newly shaved head feeling foreign under his fingertips.
3. The sun's harsh rays beat down on her exposed scalp, quickly heating her black hair.
4. Rain drops freckled his scalp, the cool sensation a sharp contrast to his heated thoughts.
5. Her scalp prickled with fear, the unknown figure looming in the shadows.
6. He could feel sweat beginning to dampen his scalp as the interview questions became more challenging.
7. "It's normal for your scalp to feel itchy after a fresh haircut," the barber explained, sweeping away the loose hairs.
8. "I think you might be having a reaction to the shampoo. Your scalp is all red," she pointed out, a note of concern in her voice.
9. She ran her fingers over her scalp, enjoying the feeling of the water washing out the conditioner.
10. He winced as the brush snagged a tangle, tugging painfully at his scalp.
11. Her scalp itched fiercely under the tight weave of her braids.
12. She could feel her scalp tingle as the cold air hit her wet hair.

Scrotum

This skin-covered sac houses and protects the testes in males hanging beneath the penis. Its primary function is to maintain an optimal temperature for sperm production.

Points of View

1. He shifted uncomfortably in his seat, the tight jeans chafing against his scrotum.
2. As he pulled on his swimming trunks, the cold fabric pressed against his scrotum, sending a shiver up his spine.
3. He felt a jolt of pain shoot through his scrotum as he landed awkwardly on the bike seat.
4. The incessant itching of his scrotum was a maddening distraction he could do without.
5. He felt a sudden, sharp pain in his scrotum as he straddled the fence.
6. A wave of relief washed over him as the doctor assured him that the lump on his scrotum was benign.
7. He scratched his scrotum surreptitiously, hoping no one would notice.
8. He adjusted his scrotum discreetly, the heat making his underwear stick uncomfortably.
9. He cringed as the soccer ball struck him in the scrotum, momentarily blinding him with pain.
10. He blushed as the doctor asked him about any scrotum abnormalities.
11. "You'll feel a slight pressure on your scrotum," the doctor warned before proceeding with the examination.
12. "Remember to wear protective gear. A hit to the scrotum can be extremely painful," the coach advised, holding up a protective cup.

Seminal Vesicles

This is a small, tube-shaped gland found near the bladder in males. It helps produce much of the fluid that mixes with sperm to form semen, which is the cloudy fluid that carries sperm.

Points of View

1. His mind was buzzing with questions about the health of his seminal vesicles after reading the doctor's report.
2. He understood that the seminal vesicles played a crucial role in reproduction, something he wished he knew earlier.
3. His knowledge about his own seminal vesicles was scant until his recent health scare forced him to learn more.
4. "The seminal vesicles produce much of the fluid found in semen," the biology teacher explained, pointing to the diagram on the whiteboard.
5. "Your seminal vesicles seem to be functioning normally," the doctor assured him after a thorough examination.
6. The patient winced as the doctor examined the area around his seminal vesicles.
7. His hand shaking slightly, he studied the ultrasound image, the seminal vesicles clearly visible.
8. The biology student sketched the seminal vesicles, trying to commit their shape to memory for his upcoming exam.
9. As he stared at the model of the male reproductive system, his attention focused on the seminal vesicles.
10. He felt a tightening in the area of his seminal vesicles, the result of the procedure he had undergone earlier.
11. The intricate structure of the seminal vesicles fascinated him, adding to his resolve to specialize in urology.
12. The surgeon's steady hands maneuvered around the seminal vesicles, a bead of sweat trickling down his forehead.

Shins

The shin is the front part of the lower leg between the knee and the ankle. It's where you'll find the shinbone, or tibia, which is the larger and stronger of the two bones in the leg below the knee.

Points of View

1. She iced her shin, hoping to alleviate some of the swelling.
2. The sharp pain in his shin made him wince, memories of his childhood soccer injuries resurfacing.
3. Her shins ached from the long hike, each step becoming more laborious than the last.
4. Feeling the cool grass against his shins, he realized how much he missed playing football.
5. "Your shin's fractured," the doctor announced, her voice grave.
6. "My shins are killing me after that workout," he complained, stretching out on the yoga mat.
7. He traced the scar running down his shin, a permanent reminder of his adventurous youth.
8. He looked down at his bruised shin, the aftermath of his clumsiness.
9. His shins bore the brunt of the impact, the bicycle skidding out of control.
10. The shin guards felt restrictive, but he knew they were necessary for his safety.
11. Despite the protective shin guards, the impact of the ball still stung.
12. She propped up her legs, resting her sore shins on the ottoman.

Shoulders

The joints where the upper arm bones (humerus), shoulder blades (scapula), and collarbone (clavicle) meet. They are one of the most movable joints in the body, allowing a wide range of motions.

Points of View

1. He felt a reassuring squeeze on his shoulder, a silent message of support from his teammate.
2. She reveled in the warmth spreading across her shoulders as the sun finally broke through the clouds.
3. The weight on his shoulders lifted as he finally shared his secret, a sigh escaping his lips.
4. She draped her coat over her shoulders, bracing herself against the chill.
5. His shoulders slumped as he processed the bad news, his spirits dampened.
6. "Your shoulders seem tense," the masseuse noted, applying more pressure.
7. "Put your shoulders back, stand tall," the dance instructor directed, demonstrating the posture.
8. He massaged his shoulders, trying to work out the knots of stress.
9. She touched her shoulder gingerly, the pain from the fall still fresh.
10. His shoulders relaxed as he heard the comforting sound of her voice.
11. The tailored jacket fit snugly on her shoulders, enhancing her confident posture.
12. She leaned her head on his shoulder, finding comfort in his presence.

Skin

Acting as the body's largest organ, the skin serves as a protective barrier against environmental hazards, helps regulate body temperature, enables the sensations of touch, heat, and cold, and aids in vitamin D production.

Points of View

1. Her skin was radiant in the morning light, glowing with health and vitality.
2. He could feel the grit of the sand against his skin, reminding him of childhood beach vacations.
3. The icy wind bit at her exposed skin, making her shiver involuntarily.
4. The cool cream soothed his sunburned skin, offering him much-needed relief.
5. "Your skin is quite dry. Try this moisturizer," the dermatologist advised, handing him a sample.
6. His hand traced the rough scar on his skin, a grim reminder of the accident.
7. A blush crept up her skin at his words, betraying her composure.
8. The sun kissed her skin, leaving her feeling warm and content.
9. "My skin is so sensitive, even the slightest touch feels like a burn," he confessed.
10. A spider skittered across her skin, sending a shiver down her spine.
11. "Try to avoid scratching. It'll only damage your skin further," her friend advised.
12. The mudpack left her skin feeling refreshed and rejuvenated.

Small Intestine

A long, highly convoluted tube in the digestive system, the small intestine absorbs about 90% of the nutrients from food. It is divided into the duodenum, the jejunum, and the ileum.

Points of View

1. His stomach churned, and he could almost feel his small intestine twisting in discomfort.
2. The diagnosis was a shock: a blockage in her small intestine that required immediate surgery.
3. "The small intestine absorbs most of the nutrients. That's why diet is so crucial," the nutritionist explained.
4. Every bite of the spicy food was a challenge to his small intestine, yet he persevered.
5. "You have a healthy small intestine, which is excellent news," the doctor announced.
6. She recalled her anatomy class, the image of the coiled small intestine still clear in her mind.
7. The cramping in his small intestine was relentless, leaving him doubled over in pain.
8. "Did you know the small intestine is about 20 feet long?" he asked, relishing her surprised expression.
9. He felt his small intestine rumble, signaling the onset of his food allergy symptoms.
10. The ultrasound showed a healthy small intestine, a relief for both her and the doctor.
11. "Remember to chew your food well. It makes it easier for your small intestine to absorb nutrients," her trainer reminded.
12. The thought of the surgery scared him, but he knew his small intestine needed it.

Sole

The sole is the bottom part of the foot that touches the ground when you stand or walk. It is made up of layers of skin, fat, and muscle, and contains numerous nerve endings. The sole helps cushion and support the weight of the body.

Points of View

1. The soles of his feet throbbed with every step on the scorching sand.
2. She felt the tickle of grass under the soles of her bare feet, taking her back to her childhood.
3. "Feels like I've walked a thousand miles," she grumbled, rubbing the sore soles of her feet.
4. His boots offered little comfort, the hard sole digging into his foot with each step.
5. "The sole of your foot has numerous pressure points. That's why foot massages feel so good," the therapist explained.
6. The cold floor was a rude awakening, the icy chill seeping into the soles of his feet.
7. She winced as a pebble stabbed the soft sole of her foot.
8. "Your shoes seem too tight. It's not good for the soles of your feet," the salesperson noted.
9. He could feel the vibrations of the music in the soles of his feet, invigorating him.
10. The blisters on the soles of her feet were painful reminders of the long journey.
11. "Try to distribute your weight evenly on the soles of your feet," the yoga instructor advised.
12. Walking barefoot, she could feel the earth's warmth radiating into the soles of her feet.

Spinal Cord

A critical part of the nervous system. This long, slender tube extends from the lower part of the brain, down the center of the back, to the waist. It serves as a link between the brain and the peripheral nervous system. The spinal cord enables you to move and to feel sensations such as touch and temperature.

Points of View

1. The impact jarred his spinal cord, sending a wave of pain up his back.
2. "The spinal cord is like the body's information highway," the teacher explained.
3. A shiver ran down her spinal cord at the eerie sound.
4. His spinal cord injury was a constant challenge, but he met it with resilience.
5. "A damaged spinal cord can lead to paralysis," the doctor said gravely.
6. The icy water sent a shock through his spinal cord, jolting him awake.
7. Every breath was a struggle, pain radiating from her spinal cord.
8. "Did you know that your spinal cord is not as long as your backbone?" he asked, enjoying her puzzled expression.
9. She could feel her spinal cord align with each yoga pose, a sense of balance settling in.
10. The X-ray showed a healthy spinal cord, much to their relief.
11. "Good posture is essential for the health of your spinal cord," the physiotherapist reminded him.
12. The dull ache in her spinal cord was a constant companion, a bitter reminder of the past.

Spleen

A soft, spongy organ located in the upper left of the abdomen, under the rib cage. It is part of the immune system and helps the body fight off infections and filter old and damaged cells out of the bloodstream.

Points of View

1. She felt a sharp pain in the area of her spleen and winced.
2. "The spleen plays a big role in fighting off infections," the doctor explained.
3. His injury had affected his spleen, complicating his recovery.
4. "I'm no doctor, but I think the spleen is around here," she said, pointing vaguely to her left side.
5. An underlying dread gnawed at him when the doctor mentioned a spleen biopsy.
6. They found her cradling her side, where the spleen was located.
7. "It's a good thing you came in when you did. Your spleen was dangerously enlarged," the doctor informed her.
8. The discomfort in her spleen area made it hard for her to focus on anything else.
9. Despite his complaints, the scans showed a perfectly healthy spleen.
10. "Did you know the spleen helps filter out old blood cells?" he asked, ever the trivia enthusiast.
11. The doctor's mention of spleen removal sent a chill down her spine.
12. His laughter was suddenly cut short by a jolt of pain in his spleen area.

Sternum

Also known as the breastbone, is a long, flat bone located in the center of the chest. It connects to the ribs with cartilage, forming the front of the rib cage, and helps protect the heart, lungs, and major blood vessels from injury.

Points of View

1. She pressed her hand to her sternum, trying to calm her racing heart.
2. "The sternum protects some of the most important organs in your body," he explained.
3. A forceful hit to the sternum winded him, making him gasp for breath.
4. "My sternum hurts every time I cough," she complained, grimacing.
5. His pulse pounded in his ears, the rapid beats echoing in his sternum.
6. She woke up with a strange discomfort in her sternum.
7. "You may feel some pressure on your sternum during this exercise," the trainer warned.
8. The impact on her sternum left her breathless and wincing in pain.
9. His sternum injury was healing, but it would take time.
10. "Did you know the sternum is sometimes called the breastbone?" she asked, sharing her newfound knowledge.
11. A coughing fit left her sternum aching and her body tired.
12. The doctor pressed gently on her sternum, asking if it caused any discomfort.

Stomach

This is a muscular organ located on the left side of the upper abdomen. It receives food from the esophagus, mixes it with gastric juices to break it into a more digestible form, and then passes it to the small intestine.

Points of View

1. His stomach churned uncomfortably at the sight of the exotic food.
2. "The stomach plays a big part in digesting your food," she explained, tapping on the diagram.
3. She felt butterflies in her stomach as she stepped onto the stage.
4. "My stomach's been upset all day," he grumbled, pressing a hand to his abdomen.
5. The punch landed squarely on his stomach, knocking the wind out of him.
6. "Remember, it's not good to go swimming right after you eat. Give your stomach time to digest," she advised.
7. The mention of her name sent a nervous jolt to her stomach.
8. The queasy feeling in his stomach persisted despite the medication.
9. "You've got a stomach of steel, eating all that spicy food!" she exclaimed, watching him in amazement.
10. Her stomach twisted into knots as she awaited the test results.
11. He patted his stomach contentedly after the satisfying meal.
12. "Trust your gut, trust your stomach instincts," he said, tapping his belly for emphasis.

Practice Exercises

Instruction: Use this exercise to deepen your understanding of the lesson after reviewing each body part, such as the Adam's Apple or zygote, or after completing all the body parts in a particular letter set—A, B, or Z.

Task 1: Tagging Dialogues: Identify and list the dialogue tags used in the examples.

Task 2: Tracking Action Beats: Analyze the provided examples and identify action beats.

Task 3: Teasing Out Narrative Styles: Review the examples and distinguish between two narrative styles. Mark instances of deep POV that immerse you in a character's emotions or thoughts with a check mark (✓). Use an asterisk (*) to denote shallow POV instances, which focus primarily on surface-level actions or descriptions.

Task 4: Testing Your Skills with New Examples: Write four new phrases or short paragraphs incorporating an action beat and a dialogue tag. Use deep and shallow POV to explore different aspects of the body part discussed in this section.

Teeth

The hard, bony structures in the mouth that play a crucial role in chewing food and aiding speech. They help break down food for digestion and help in forming certain sounds when speaking.

Points of View

1. Jake ran his tongue over his teeth, the taste of mint toothpaste still lingering.
2. "Dentist," she thought, the word tasting metallic on her tongue against the dull throb of a rebellious tooth. It pulsed in a counterpoint to her racing heart, an insistent drumbeat demanding attention.
3. He bared his teeth in a grin, feeling victorious.
4. Sarah brushed her teeth meticulously, removing every trace of dinner.
5. A white-hot spike of pain lanced through his jaw, radiating outwards in waves. His breath hitched, and a gasp caught between clenched teeth. Each pulse echoed in the throbbing nerve, a maddening rhythm miming his frantic heartbeat.
6. "The apple is so crisp," he commented, crunching into it, teeth slicing through the fruit with ease.
7. As she sipped her coffee, the heat made her sensitive teeth tingle.
8. He gnawed on the pen, teeth leaving tiny indentations on the plastic.
9. The cold ice cream made her teeth ache as she took a bite.
10. "You have something in your teeth," she pointed out, her teeth flashing white as she grinned.
11. She clenched her teeth as she received the bill, the price higher than she expected.
12. He flossed his teeth before bed, a part of his nightly routine.

Temples

These are sensitive, flat regions on the sides of the forehead, located behind the eyes and nestled between the forehead and the ears. While they do not perform a specific function, the temples cover the temporal bones situated just beneath the skin. These bones are crucial for various aspects of head anatomy.

Points of View

1. A vein throbbed in his temple, the stress mounting.
2. "My head is pounding," she said, fingers massaging her temples.
3. He could feel a bead of sweat trickle down his temple.
4. Rubbing her temples, she tried to stave off the impending migraine.
5. A lock of hair kept falling over his temple, tickling his skin.
6. "It's just so loud," she complained, pressing her palms against her temples.
7. The warmth of the sun on his temples felt soothing.
8. His brow crinkled in concentration, the crease on his temple seeming to etch deeper with each passing moment.
9. The chill of the glass pressed against her temple, its cold touch seeping in and dispersing the tendrils of her throbbing headache.
10. Her fingers adjusted the frame of her glasses, its rigid edge pressing into the softness of her temples.
11. A mosquito whirred in a maddening circle near his temple, its relentless, high-pitched drone needling at his patience.
12. His fingers brushed the purpling bruise on his temple, a sharp intake of breath at the flare of tenderness.

Testes

Also known as testicles, the testes are male reproductive organs responsible for producing sperm and hormones like testosterone. This role is crucial for male fertility and the development of male physical characteristics.

Points of View

1. His testes hummed with a lingering discomfort, an internal echo of his unfortunate cycling mishap.
2. He shifted, trying to alleviate the squeeze against his testes, the tight jeans becoming a denim vise he regretted wearing.
3. A sharp pain in his testes made him double over.
4. He cupped his testes protectively as the ball whizzed past him.
5. His testes ached from the long bike ride.
6. He winced, feeling the impact in his testes.
7. The doctor's professional touch roved over his testes, part of the routine check-up, yet an intrusion he never quite got used to.
8. He could feel the warmth of the bathwater soothing his testes.
9. "You need to check your testes regularly for any changes," the doctor instructed.
10. An uncomfortable twinge sparked in his testes, an intimate alarm bell echoing his escalating anxiety.
11. His testes felt heavy, an indication of his arousal.
12. He sighed in relief as his testes escaped the constriction of his underwear.

Thighs

The thighs are the parts of the human body between the hips and the knees. They contain the largest bone in the human body, the femur.

Points of View

1. The scorch of overworked muscles clawed up her thighs, a fiery protest from her body that she had pushed too far this time.
2. The pulse of the bassline thrummed under his palm as he drummed it on his thigh, his body syncing with the infectious rhythm.
3. The cat curled on his thigh, the tickle of its fur prickling his skin and sending tiny sparks of affection coursing through him.
4. "I'm so cold," she muttered, her hands vigorously rubbing her thighs, trying to kindle warmth on her icy skin.
5. Rain-soaked denim clung to his thighs like a second skin, every squelch a cold, wet reminder of the downpour he'd endured.
6. Frustration seared through her, her palm connecting with her thigh in a slap of disbelief. Could her luck get any worse?
7. The cool kiss of the leather car seat seeped through his pants, its chill encasing his thighs with each passing second.
8. His thighs gripped the horse, muscles strained taut, holding onto the powerful animal beneath him as if his life depended on it.
9. Her thighs throbbed in sync with her frustration, the confined space of the airplane seat turning into a mini torture chamber.
10. His mother's thigh became his safe haven, the toddler clutching it with chubby fingers as he peeked at the world with shy curiosity.

11. His laptop teetered on his thigh, the keys clicking under his fingers in a rhythmic symphony of productivity.
12. A nervous check on her thigh found the earlier glaring bruise now a faded memory, a wave of relief washing over her.

Throat

This is the front part of the neck, starting from the back of the mouth and going down to the top of the chest. It includes the pharynx and larynx, which help us swallow, speak, and breathe.

Points of View

1. His throat tightened, and a lump formed, making it difficult to swallow. He blinked back tears, feeling the words stick.
2. She took a bite and immediately coughed, clutching her throat. "It's just so spicy," she gasped, tears in her eyes.
3. Her throat was parched, and the icy drink felt soothing as it washed down. She closed her eyes, savoring the cool relief.
4. He cleared his throat, a nervous flutter in his stomach, gathering the courage to speak up. "I have something to say," he finally stammered.
5. Laughter bubbled from her throat, infectious and light. She leaned back, eyes twinkling. "I can't believe you did that!" she exclaimed.
6. "My throat feels so dry," he complained, coughing into his elbow, reaching for his glass of water.
7. The scream lodged in her throat, a silent plea for help. She froze, eyes wide, and her mind screaming what her voice couldn't.
8. She ran her fingers down her throat, following the delicate chain of her necklace. "It was my grandmother's," she whispered, lost in memory.
9. His voice echoed in the room, deep, and originating from his broad throat. "I won't allow it," he declared, his tone unyielding.
10. "I can't breathe," he wheezed, hand clutching at his constricting throat, panic in his eyes.

11. He swallowed hard, the bitterness still lingering in his throat. "That's awful," he muttered, grimacing.

12. She gulped down the glass of water, her throat demanding hydration. "Finally," she sighed, placing the empty glass on the table.

Thymus Gland

This gland is in the upper chest, just above the heart, which is very important for the body's defense against illness. It helps develop special white blood cells called T-lymphocytes, which fight off infections.

Points of View

1. He marveled at how the thymus gland worked, a silent army creator within the body.
2. He remembered studying about the thymus gland in medical school, how it worked tirelessly to protect the body.
3. "The thymus gland is crucial in our fight against infections," the lecturer pointed out.
4. He pointed to the diagram, showing the class where the thymus gland was located.
5. "The thymus gland is an underappreciated part of our immune system," the doctor mused.
6. The doctor explained the role of the thymus gland in the immune response.
7. She admired the body's intricate design, especially the often-overlooked thymus gland.
8. He touched his chest, wondering about the hidden thymus gland inside.
9. Reading about the thymus gland, she was in awe of the body's defense mechanism.
10. The research paper detailed the fascinating workings of the thymus gland.
11. As a science teacher, he always highlighted the importance of the thymus gland in immunity.
12. She took a deep breath, aware of her thymus gland silently protecting her.

Thyroid Gland

This small, butterfly-shaped gland is found at the base of the neck. It makes hormones that control metabolism, which is how the body uses energy and helps keep its activities balanced.

Points of View

1. The cold press of the doctor's stethoscope against her neck brought an unsettling focus to her thyroid gland, the culprit of her recent weight fluctuations.
2. She swallowed nervously, suddenly aware of the tiny, butterfly-shaped thyroid gland inside her neck.
3. The lump in her throat had nothing to do with emotion; it was an alarming reminder of her swollen thyroid gland.
4. In the quiet of his office, he reviewed the data on thyroid gland disorders, his mind buzzing with possible solutions.
5. He swallowed his medication, a daily necessity to keep his misbehaving thyroid gland in check.
6. He ran a finger lightly along the base of his neck, a silent prayer for his overworked thyroid gland.
7. "The thyroid gland plays a critical role in our body's metabolism," the professor explained, drawing a diagram on the board.
8. When she thought about it, it was strange how such a small gland like the thyroid could hold so much control over her body.
9. From her biology class, she remembered how the thyroid gland functioned, a silent regulator in the complex human body.
10. He tapped the base of his neck, trying to pinpoint the location of his thyroid gland.

11. She tried to visualize her thyroid gland, the silent overseer of her body's energy usage.
12. "Your thyroid gland seems to be underactive," the doctor commented, her eyes focused on the test results.

Toenails

These are the hard, protective covers on the upper surfaces of the ends of the toes. They are made of a tough protein called keratin, which helps protect the sensitive tips of the toes.

Points of View

1. The pink polish on her toenails had started to chip, a stark contrast to her otherwise meticulous appearance.
2. He absentmindedly picked at his toenails, his mind far away from the task at hand.
3. "I'm thinking of getting a pedicure," she commented, inspecting her bare toenails.
4. The pain was immediate and sharp as he stubbed his toe, his toenail bearing the brunt of the impact.
5. He looked down at his toenails, deciding it was finally time to trim them.
6. She admired her freshly painted toenails, a pop of color against the dull winter backdrop.
7. Her toenail caught onto the seam of her sock, an annoying reminder of her procrastination to cut it.
8. As a long-distance runner, he gave his toenails extra attention to prevent discomfort.
9. "These boots are killing my toes," she winced, imagining her poor toenails squeezed against the leather.
10. Her son's toenails were growing so quickly, another sign of how fast he was growing.
11. He cringed at the sight of the bruise under his toenail, a painful souvenir from his hike.
12. She pulled off her socks, revealing her toenails decorated with little sunflowers.

Toes

Digits of the foot, usually five per foot, that help maintain balance while standing and walking.

Points of View

1. He curled his toes into the soft carpet, trying to ground himself in the overwhelming situation.
2. His frosty toes, numb from the winter chill, longed for the warmth of his heated boots.
3. "Mind your toes," she warned, swinging the heavy box through the narrow hallway.
4. Her smallest toe, smacked hard against the doorframe, throbbed with sharp, sudden pain.
5. A sliver of cool air danced between my toes, sending a shiver up my leg. The open-toed sandals offered a glimpse of my handiwork - a cheerful riot of color on each carefully painted toenail.
6. He stared at his bare toes, wiggling them against the cool bed sheets.
7. "Always land on the balls of your feet," the coach explained, pointing at his toes for emphasis.
8. The grass, cool and damp under her bare toes, was a refreshing break from the city's hot asphalt.
9. He gingerly prodded his swollen toe, wincing at the burst of pain.
10. "Don't step on my toes!" she shrieked, hopping away from his clumsy feet.
11. The sensation of cold water lapping against his toes instantly put his mind at ease.
12. Sand squeezed between her toes, a tangible reminder of her long-awaited beach vacation.

Tongue

This muscular organ in the mouth is crucial for tasting, speaking, and swallowing. It helps us enjoy flavors, communicate through speech, and move food effectively to the throat.

Points of View

1. The tangy taste of lemon burst onto her tongue, a reminder of her grandmother's homemade lemonade.
2. His tongue felt dry and thick in his mouth, a testament to his nervousness.
3. "My tongue's gone numb," he complained, swirling the ice cube around his mouth.
4. The spicy flavor set her tongue ablaze, much more intense than she had anticipated.
5. His tongue tripped over the foreign words, struggling to keep up with the fast-paced conversation.
6. "I bit my tongue," she muttered, wincing at the metallic taste of blood in her mouth.
7. The ice cream melted on her tongue, a sweet relief from the summer heat.
8. His tongue clicked against the roof of his mouth, a habitual sound when he was deep in thought.
9. She poked her tongue out in concentration, focused on her intricate painting.
10. The word sat heavy on her tongue, a secret she wasn't ready to share.
11. He stuck out his tongue, concentrating on the difficult jigsaw puzzle before him.
12. "You've got a sharp tongue," she retorted, stung by his harsh words.

Tonsils

These are oval-shaped, soft tissue masses located at the very back of the mouth on either side of the throat, also known as the palatine tonsils. They help fight infections as part of the immune system.

Points of View

1. The aching pain radiated from her tonsils, a throbbing beat matching her heart.
2. His swollen tonsils made swallowing a torturous ordeal, his throat protesting with every gulp.
3. "Can't speak," she whispered, pointing at her inflamed tonsils.
4. Her tonsils, once guardians against infections, were now an enemy that needed removal.
5. His tonsils were unremarkable, unlike his childhood memories of repeated bouts of tonsillitis.
6. "You've got some inflamed tonsils," the doctor noted, shining a light into her open mouth.
7. The taste of the medicinal spray brought instant relief to her sore tonsils.
8. Every cough, every scratchy whisper, was a reminder of his tonsil surgery.
9. "Ice cream diet starts today," he grinned, his tonsils freshly removed.
10. The smooth, cold popsicle soothed her tonsils, a beacon of relief amid the pain.
11. He grimaced at his reflection, his tonsils looking like crimson bulbs set in a pink field.
12. "Be brave," she murmured to herself, swallowing past the discomfort of her infected tonsils.

Torso

Also known as the trunk, this central part of the body supports the neck and limbs and houses vital organs, including the heart, lungs, and stomach. It is key in maintaining the body's core structure and function.

Points of View

1. A chill ran down her torso, her shirt damp from the sudden rain.
2. His torso was a canvas of tattoos, each one narrating a different story.
3. "I'm so full," he groaned, patting his swollen torso.
4. The weight of her safety gear pressed against her torso, a constant reminder of the danger she faced.
5. He absently traced the scar running down his torso, a memento of a forgotten battle.
6. "Hold it right there," she instructed, guiding his hands to the right spot on her torso.
7. The soft fabric of her dress hugged her torso, making her feel beautiful and confident.
8. His lean torso moved gracefully as he danced, capturing the attention of the crowd.
9. "It's freezing!" he exclaimed, submerging his torso into the icy water.
10. She cradled her torso protectively, the pain from her injury was becoming unbearable.
11. He admired his toned torso in the mirror, the result of months of diligent workouts.
12. "I'm tired," she declared, flopping down onto the sofa, her torso sinking into the plush cushions.

Trachea

Also known as the windpipe, this tube connects the pharynx and larynx to the lungs. It keeps air flowing freely in and out of the lungs for efficient respiration.

Points of View

1. She struggled to draw in a breath, her trachea feeling constricted, as if it were bound by invisible cords.
2. His laugh bubbled up, echoing warmly from his trachea.
3. "Inhale deeply," the doctor instructed, listening to the air whistling through her trachea.
4. A harsh cough rattled her trachea, each bout feeling like a storm wreaking havoc.
5. His trachea worked rhythmically, the steady cadence of his calm breathing.
6. "It's just a small nick," he shrugged, pointing at the bandage placed close to his trachea.
7. The sting of cold air hit her trachea with each panting breath, serving as a harsh reminder of the frigid weather.
8. He watched his daughter's trachea bob gently as she swallowed her first bite of solid food.
9. "Don't speak," she warned him, her hand hovering protectively near his newly operated trachea.
10. Her pulse hammered in her trachea, each beat echoing the terror she was trying to swallow down.
11. His trachea moved rhythmically, the visible proof of his calm, steady breathing.
12. "No more talking," the doctor ordered, his eyes drawn to the surgical scar on her trachea.

Practice Exercises

Instruction: Use this exercise to deepen your understanding of the lesson after reviewing each body part, such as the Adam's Apple or zygote, or after completing all the body parts in a particular letter set—A, B, or Z.

Task 1: Tagging Dialogues: Identify and list the dialogue tags used in the examples.

Task 2: Tracking Action Beats: Analyze the provided examples and identify action beats.

Task 3: Teasing Out Narrative Styles: Review the examples and distinguish between two narrative styles. Mark instances of deep POV that immerse you in a character's emotions or thoughts with a check mark (✓). Use an asterisk (*) to denote shallow POV instances, which focus primarily on surface-level actions or descriptions.

Task 4: Testing Your Skills with New Examples: Write four new phrases or short paragraphs incorporating an action beat and a dialogue tag. Use deep and shallow POV to explore different aspects of the body part discussed in this section.

Ureters

These tubes transport urine from the kidneys, where it is produced, to the bladder, where it is stored before being expelled from the body.

Points of View

1. After a lengthy procedure, the doctors managed to remove the kidney stone lodged in her left ureter.
2. He felt unusual discomfort and pressure in his lower back, perhaps an issue with his ureter.
3. The surgeon navigated the tiny camera, inspecting the right ureter for signs of abnormality.
4. "The pain seems to be around the area of your ureters," the doctor stated, reviewing the ultrasound results.
5. Ureters serve an important function, but we seldom acknowledge their role.
6. The medical illustration highlighted the ureters, demonstrating their critical function.
7. "Can you point to where your ureter is?" the anatomy teacher asked the class, referring to either side.
8. He had never considered his ureters until that sharp, unmistakable pain had him crumpled on the floor.
9. She read about ureters in the biology book, amazed at how meticulously our bodies work.
10. The doctor showed them a model indicating the path of the ureters.
11. That ache in her side, she was convinced it had something to do with her ureters, the relentless pain akin to a flame slowly growing.
12. A nagging pain stirred, a discordant note in his body's harmonious symphony. It echoed from his ureters, a soft yet insistent plea for attention.

Urethra

This tube carries urine from the bladder to the outside of the body. In males, it also serves the dual purpose of transporting semen.

Points of View

1. After the accident, he had to use a catheter to bypass his urethra.
2. The doctor explained how the catheter would be inserted into the patient's urethra.
3. "The bacteria entered through the urethra and caused the infection," the doctor said, detailing the cause of the UTI.
4. In a male's body, the urethra serves a dual purpose for the expulsion of urine and semen.
5. The doctor pointed to the urethra on the anatomical diagram during the health class.
6. "The swelling might cause difficulty in passing urine due to the narrowing of the urethra," the nurse explained.
7. The anatomical differences between the male and female urethra contribute to varying susceptibility to urinary tract infections.
8. The medical student held the model, examining the urethra structure carefully.
9. His urethra stung like fire, the punishment for his questionable decisions last night.
10. The pain was sharp and burning, the sensation of a thousand tiny knives slicing through her urethra.
11. She felt the stinging sensation retreat, her urethra seemingly in a ceasefire with her body's attackers.
12. The sensation was akin to a desert trek, each drop of urine an oasis escaping through her parched urethra.

Uterus

A major female reproductive organ, responsive to hormones and commonly known as the womb, where a fetus grows during pregnancy. It includes the myometrium, a muscular layer essential for contractions and supporting the pregnancy.

Points of View

1. The uterus contracts during childbirth, pushing the baby through the birth canal.
2. When the doctor told her the uterus was healthy, she exhaled a sigh of relief.
3. There was a longing within her, a deep-seated desire nestled in her uterus for a life not yet conceived.
4. "The ultrasound shows a small fibroid in your uterus," the doctor explained, her face professional but empathetic.
5. The surgeon examined the monitor, guiding the tiny camera to view the patient's uterus.
6. Every cramp was a reminder of her womanhood, her uterus conspiring with nature's monthly cycle.
7. The teacher pointed at the diagram of the uterus, explaining the stages of the menstrual cycle.
8. "Endometriosis can cause tissue to grow outside the uterus," the doctor said, his voice laced with compassion.
9. A hysterectomy involves the surgical removal of the uterus.
10. The news of the impending removal of her uterus weighed on her like a tombstone, burying her dreams of motherhood.
11. She ran her fingers over the barely visible scar, a reminder of her once-occupied uterus.
12. Her uterus was a nest woven of love and dreams, waiting for a miracle to dwell.

Practice Exercises

Instruction: Use this exercise to deepen your understanding of the lesson after reviewing each body part, such as the Adam's Apple or zygote, or after completing all the body parts in a particular letter set—A, B, or Z.

Task 1: Tagging Dialogues: Identify and list the dialogue tags used in the examples.

Task 2: Tracking Action Beats: Analyze the provided examples and identify action beats.

Task 3: Teasing Out Narrative Styles: Review the examples and distinguish between two narrative styles. Mark instances of deep POV that immerse you in a character's emotions or thoughts with a check mark (✓). Use an asterisk (*) to denote shallow POV instances, which focus primarily on surface-level actions or descriptions.

Task 4: Testing Your Skills with New Examples: Write four new phrases or short paragraphs incorporating an action beat and a dialogue tag. Use deep and shallow POV to explore different aspects of the body part discussed in this section.

Vagina

An internal sexual organ in females that serves multiple functions: it is the canal through which childbirth occurs, the pathway for menstrual flow from the uterus, and the route for sperm to reach the egg. It also plays a crucial role in sexual intercourse.

Points of View

1. A familiar itch crept down there, a prickling sensation that sent a wave of annoyance through me. Was it that time again? Peeking into the mirror, I braced myself for the telltale signs – a confirmation that my vagina was waging war against itself with an overgrowth of yeast.
2. Her vagina was a sacred temple, the gatekeeper of life and pleasure.
3. "The vagina is self-cleaning," explained the health teacher, navigating the awkwardness of the class.
4. She felt a twinge of discomfort in her vagina, a familiar sign of her impending period.
5. The midwife encouraged her to breathe, her expert hands ready to guide the baby from the vagina.
6. "Your vagina is perfectly normal," the doctor assured, easing her insecurities.
7. Waves of pressure crashed against my core, an insistent urge pushing downwards. My breath hitched in staccato gasps as the muscles in my vagina stretched and contracted, a primal rhythm urging the miracle of life outwards.
8. He gently examined the model of the vagina, studying for his medical exam.
9. She was a woman in full bloom, her vagina a garden of mysteries yet to be explored.

10. A familiar itch crept down there, a prickling sensation that sent a wave of annoyance through me. Was it that time again? Peeking into the mirror, I braced myself for the telltale signs – a confirmation that my vagina was waging war against itself with an overgrowth of yeast.

11. As the contractions hit, she could feel her vagina preparing to bring forth life.

12. Brea paused, tracing the rim of her coffee mug with a tentative finger. "It's not just about reproduction," she whispered, her voice carrying a mix of vulnerability and enlightenment. "It's as if every part of you is acknowledged, even celebrated." She leaned back, her eyes revealing a profound realization. "The vagina isn't just a pathway; it's a place where pleasure and love intertwine uniquely."

Vas Deferens

The vas deferens are long, muscular tubes that are a part of the male reproductive system, responsible for transporting sperm from the epididymis in anticipation of ejaculation.

Points of View

1. "The vas deferens are a crucial part of the male reproductive system," the biology teacher explained.
2. She pointed to the diagram, tracing the path of the vas deferens with her finger.
3. The vasectomy procedure involved cutting and sealing the vas deferens.
4. He could hardly believe the intricate nature of the vas deferens, carrying potential life within their slender tubes.
5. Blockage in the vas deferens can cause male infertility.
6. Knowing he was about to become a father, he was more conscious of the silent workings of his vas deferens.
7. The textbook showed a detailed image of the vas deferens, labeled and color-coded for the students' benefit.
8. His choice to undergo a vasectomy, to sever his vas deferens, had been a heavy one.
9. The surgeon prepared to operate, about to interrupt the journey of countless sperm in the vas deferens.
10. "Without the vas deferens, the sperm would have no route to follow," the professor lectured.
11. The vas deferens plays a crucial role in male sexual reproduction.
12. The vas deferens, like secretive conduits, carried the potential for life in the form of microscopic swimmers.

Veins

Blood vessels that typically carry deoxygenated blood from various parts of the body back to the heart. An exception is the pulmonary veins, which carry oxygenated blood from the lungs to the heart.

Points of View

1. She gently squeezed the crook of her elbow, making the veins prominent for the nurse.
2. "Your veins are working hard to return blood to your heart," the doctor reassured him.
3. The greenish-blue veins were visible through her thin, pale skin.
4. He noticed the veins standing out on his forearms after the strenuous workout.
5. The icy fear seemed to freeze the blood in his veins.
6. He was intrigued by the complex network of veins visible on the back of his hand.
7. As she squeezed her eyes shut, she could almost feel the rush of blood in her veins, a testament to her raging anxiety.
8. The nurse deftly inserted the needle into one of her bulging veins.
9. A sense of thrill raced through her veins as she peered over the edge of the cliff.
10. He traced his finger along the prominent veins on his arm.
11. "Veins are like highways for blood, carrying it back to your heart," the teacher explained.
12. Like rivers in the landscape of flesh, her veins pulsed with life.

Voice

The sound produced by the vibration of the vocal cords during speech. It is a powerful communication tool, expressing not only words but also a range of emotional nuances. Each person's voice is unique, reflecting individual physical and emotional states.

Points of View

1. His voice held an edge of authority that silenced the room.
2. Her voice, a lullaby to his anxiety, soothed his spiraling thoughts.
3. He raised his voice over the din of the crowd to make himself heard.
4. "We must stand up for ourselves," she said, her voice steady and strong.
5. Her voice, once a source of solace, was now just an echo in his lonely world.
6. His booming voice filled the theater, commanding the attention of the audience.
7. She found her voice again, her words slicing through the tense silence.
8. Fear constricted her throat, turning her voice into a thin whisper.
9. The warmth of his voice spread through the cold room like a cozy blanket.
10. Her voice wavered as she recounted the incident, the tremor belying her attempted composure.
11. "I won't back down," he declared, the conviction in his voice infectious.
12. His voice was the symphony to her dance of life, each word a note strung on the melody of their shared existence.

Note: In creative writing, "voice" extends beyond its literal meaning to embody a character or author's distinctive style or perspective. Its inclusion here acknowledges its significance in expressing character and advancing narrative despite not being a tangible body part. You can use other intangible aspects of the body in your creative work.

Practice Exercises

Instruction: Use this exercise to deepen your understanding of the lesson after reviewing each body part, such as the Adam's Apple or zygote, or after completing all the body parts in a particular letter set—A, B, or Z.

Task 1: Tagging Dialogues: Identify and list the dialogue tags used in the examples.

Task 2: Tracking Action Beats: Analyze the provided examples and identify action beats.

Task 3: Teasing Out Narrative Styles: Review the examples and distinguish between two narrative styles. Mark instances of deep POV that immerse you in a character's emotions or thoughts with a check mark (✓). Use an asterisk (*) to denote shallow POV instances, which focus primarily on surface-level actions or descriptions.

Task 4: Testing Your Skills with New Examples: Write four new phrases or short paragraphs incorporating an action beat and a dialogue tag. Use deep and shallow POV to explore different aspects of the body part discussed in this section.

Windpipe

A tube-shaped airway located in the throat that carries air from the nose and mouth to the lungs. It acts like a highway for air, facilitating the process of breathing in and out.

Points of View

1. He had a distinct scratch in his windpipe, a remnant of his recent cold.
2. Each breath was a battle, the air scraping its way down her windpipe, making her cough.
3. He cleared his windpipe before starting his speech, his voice echoing through the auditorium.
4. "I can't breathe," she choked out, clutching her windpipe.
5. The cold air was sharp, stinging his windpipe as he gasped for breath.
6. She felt something lodged in her windpipe, cutting off her air.
7. A fit of coughing seized him, his windpipe rattling like an old engine.
8. "It's like breathing fire," he rasped, clutching his irritated windpipe.
9. Her laughter bubbled up, tickling her windpipe before bursting forth into the room.
10. His windpipe felt tight, constricting with the intensity of his anxiety.
11. She took a deep breath, feeling the cool air fill her windpipe, a sense of calm washing over her.
12. His windpipe was a hollow echo of regret, each breath whispering the words he failed to utter.

Practice Exercises

Instruction: Use this exercise to deepen your understanding of the lesson after reviewing each body part, such as the Adam's Apple or zygote, or after completing all the body parts in a particular letter set—A, B, or Z.

Task 1: Tagging Dialogues: Identify and list the dialogue tags used in the examples.

Task 2: Tracking Action Beats: Analyze the provided examples and identify action beats.

Task 3: Teasing Out Narrative Styles: Review the examples and distinguish between two narrative styles. Mark instances of deep POV that immerse you in a character's emotions or thoughts with a check mark (✓). Use an asterisk (*) to denote shallow POV instances, which focus primarily on surface-level actions or descriptions.

Task 4: Testing Your Skills with New Examples: Write four new phrases or short paragraphs incorporating an action beat and a dialogue tag. Use deep and shallow POV to explore different aspects of the body part discussed in this section.

Xiphoid Process

This small, triangular bone or cartilage structure is located at the center of the chest, just below the lower part of the sternum. It connects to essential muscles like the diaphragm, which aids breathing, and the rectus abdominis, commonly known as the abs.

Points of View

1. A jolt of pain ripped through my lower chest. It felt like someone had stabbed me right where my ribs met my stomach. I gasped, doubling over and clutching my xiphoid process.

2. Dr. Ellis gently tapped a spot on her elderly patient's lower sternum. "This," she explained kindly to Mrs. Foxy Pierce, "is your xiphoid process. It's named after the Greek word for 'straight sword,' which fits well since it has a pointed tip." Foxy chuckled softly, her fingers brushing the spot with curiosity. "It's quite literal, isn't it?"

3. "I watch as you hunch over, a sharp pain lancing through your gut. It seems to be coming from the pointy tip of your breastbone, right below your ribs," said Sage, "That must be your xiphoid process!"

4. The blow landed squarely on Alex's xiphoid process. He winced, his breath catching in his throat. The pain was like a hot poker jabbed into his lower abdomen.

5. The punch connected with a sickening thud, sending a jolt of pain through Alex's xiphoid process.

6. "Ugh," Marah grunted, clutching her xiphoid process. "That really hurt!"

7. "It feels like someone stabbed my xiphoid process!" Alex exclaimed, wincing in pain.

8. The blow landed with a thud. "My xiphoid process!" Alex yelled, clutching his lower chest.

9. Okay, deep breaths. It's just a bruise. Maybe. That sharp sting below your ribs, where your breastbone ends, must be your xiphoid process.

10. With a choked gasp, Marah slammed into the wall, the impact sending a white-hot pain through her xiphoid process. "Ow!" she yelped, clutching her lower sternum.

11. "Oof!" I winced, the wind knocked out of me. My hand instinctively flew to my xiphoid process, where a dull ache bloomed.

12. Alex stumbled back, a surprised grunt escaping his lips. He pressed a hand to his xiphoid process, where a red welt was already blossoming. "That wasn't funny, Rylan!" he exclaimed, rubbing the sore spot.

Practice Exercises

Instruction: Use this exercise to deepen your understanding of the lesson after reviewing each body part, such as the Adam's Apple or zygote, or after completing all the body parts in a particular letter set—A, B, or Z.

Task 1: Tagging Dialogues: Identify and list the dialogue tags used in the examples.

Task 2: Tracking Action Beats: Analyze the provided examples and identify action beats.

Task 3: Teasing Out Narrative Styles: Review the examples and distinguish between two narrative styles. Mark instances of deep POV that immerse you in a character's emotions or thoughts with a check mark (✓). Use an asterisk (*) to denote shallow POV instances, which focus primarily on surface-level actions or descriptions.

Task 4: Testing Your Skills with New Examples: Write four new phrases or short paragraphs incorporating an action beat and a dialogue tag. Use deep and shallow POV to explore different aspects of the body part discussed in this section.

Y-Tendon

A Y-tendon is a type of tendon that splits into a Y-shape, allowing one muscle to attach to two separate points on a bone. This design facilitates complex movements. A typical example is the biceps Y-tendon, which connects to the radius and ulna bones in the forearm, enabling flexion and rotation. Another example includes the hamstrings in the thigh, which help bend the knee.

Points of View

1. "See this movement?" he explained to his friend while demonstrating again. "That's my extensor muscle at work, helped by a special Y-tendon connected to it. The tendon splits and attaches to the radius and ulna, the two bones in my forearm, which lets me straighten my arm and turn my hand up easily.

2. As she curled the dumbbells towards her chest, she could almost feel the Y-tendon in her biceps stretch and contract, a testament to her body's marvelous design.

3. He winced slightly, the Y-tendon in his forearm pulsing with each twist of the screwdriver, reminding him of his physical limits.

4. Sage bent and then straightened her wrist, demonstrating the smooth movement. "See how I can do this?" she asked, her voice filled with a mix of wonder and pride. "The flexors help me bend my wrist, while the extensors help straighten it out. They work together seamlessly, all thanks to a special Y-tendon connecting them to my bones."

5. She extended her leg behind her in the yoga pose, keenly aware of how the Y-tendon of her hamstrings tautly facilitated the movement.

6. A melody filled the room as Sage's fingers danced across the piano keys. "Beautiful," she whispered, lost in the music, aware that the Y-tendon in her extensor carpi ulnaris was crucial for the intricate wrist movements necessary for a flawless performance.

7. As she practiced her violin, the subtle rotations of her wrist brought attention to the Y-tendon, a silent partner in her musical expression.

8. When you bend your elbow, you can see the Y-tendon at work; it's like watching human mechanics in action.

9. "Extensor carpi radialis brevis! Where is that?" she asked. Missy smiled and pointed to her forearm. "See how the muscles bulge a bit here, near the elbow? That's where the extensor carpi radialis brevis originates. It's a little muscle running down your arm and becomes part of the Y-tendon at your wrist."

10. His gesture was smooth and controlled, hiding a symphony beneath the surface. His forearm muscles, the extensor carpi radialis, and ulnaris played a silent sonata. Each fiber tightened in perfect harmony, conducting power through the Y-tendon, the maestro of his grip. "Nice to meet you," he said with a warm smile, the hidden orchestra of his handshake known only to his body.

11. With each delicate brushstroke, Missy felt a subtle connection in her hand. "Just a touch more blue," she muttered under her breath, the Y-tendon in her extensor carpi radialis brevis providing the precise control needed to bring her artistic vision to life.

12. A silent partner joins the concerto in my arms. The extensor carpi ulnaris, working in harmony with its brevis counterpart, bending the wrist backward. Together, they extend their melody down to the wrist, adding a touch of ulnar flair to the Y-tendon's symphony.

Practice Exercises

Instruction: Use this exercise to deepen your understanding of the lesson after reviewing each body part, such as the Adam's Apple or zygote, or after completing all the body parts in a particular letter set—A, B, or Z.

Task 1: Tagging Dialogues: Identify and list the dialogue tags used in the examples.

Task 2: Tracking Action Beats: Analyze the provided examples and identify action beats.

Task 3: Teasing Out Narrative Styles: Review the examples and distinguish between two narrative styles. Mark instances of deep POV that immerse you in a character's emotions or thoughts with a check mark (✓). Use an asterisk (*) to denote shallow POV instances, which focus primarily on surface-level actions or descriptions.

Task 4: Testing Your Skills with New Examples: Write four new phrases or short paragraphs incorporating an action beat and a dialogue tag. Use deep and shallow POV to explore different aspects of the body part discussed in this section.

Zygomatic Bone

The zygomatic bone, commonly known as the cheekbone, is a prominent part of the facial skeleton. It resides on each side of the face, forming the prominence below the eye and contributing to the orbital cavity that houses the eyeball.

Points of View

1. Missy touched her cheek lightly, feeling the ridge of her zygomatic bone. "This is what gives our faces shape," she mused quietly while studying her reflection.
2. As the artist sculpted, he focused intently on the zygomatic bone. "This bone right here," he explained to his apprentice, "is what frames the entire face."
3. The blow to his cheek was sharp, sending a throbbing pain through his zygomatic bone. He grimaced, thinking, "That's going to swell tomorrow."
4. "Notice how the zygomatic bone creates the contour of the face," the makeup artist said, highlighting just below her client's eye.
5. During the anatomy class, the professor pointed out, "The zygomatic bone here is crucial for the structure of the face."
6. "Your zygomatic bone is quite pronounced; it really defines your face," remarked the photographer, adjusting the lighting to capture the model's high cheekbones.
7. Judas laughed, his zygomatic bones lifting with his smile, making his eyes crinkle at the corners.
8. He winced as the baseball narrowly missed his cheek, instinctively protecting his zygomatic bone with his glove.
9. Missy applied blush directly on her zygomatic bones, enhancing their natural prominence.
10. "Can you feel this?" the doctor asked, gently pressing on her zygomatic bone to check for misalignment.

11. "Your zygomatic bones are quite symmetrical," noted the surgeon, examining the 3D scans before the procedure.
12. In facial reconstructive surgery, the zygomatic bone's alignment is critical for both aesthetic and functional recovery.

Zygote

A zygote is a unique single cell that marks the beginning of a new life. It forms when two other special cells, a sperm, and an egg, join. This tiny cell eventually divides and grows into a complete baby.

Points of View

1. Wow, I'm a zygote! Why is it so dark and quiet here? Yet, I feel a surge of energy. I can almost sense all the possibilities ahead of me becoming a baby, playing peek-a-boo, taking my first steps.

2. The sperm and egg collided in a microscopic dance, their genetic material merging to form a single cell – the zygote. It was a tiny spark of life, invisible to the naked eye but holding the potential for something extraordinary.

3. Freya Bierhaals felt a flutter of hope deep within her. The doctor had confirmed it – a tiny zygote had formed, a testament to the miracle of life.

4. "Congratulations!" the doctor beamed. A wave of relief washes over you as you hear the news – there's a tiny zygote nestled inside you, ready to begin its incredible journey.

5. Just a tiny speck, but I'm filled with instructions! This code will guide me as I divide and grow, transforming into something extraordinary.

6. "It's a miracle," he whispers, gazing at the ultrasound screen. A tiny flicker on the image represents the zygote, a symbol of hope and the start of something beautiful.

7. "We did it!" the scientists cheered, their years of research culminating in this moment. A single, healthy zygote pulsed on the screen – a testament to their dedication and the power of science.

8. Freya watched the magnified image of the zygote on the screen, her heart swelling with emotion. "That's the start of a new life," she whispered, awed by the single cell that would become her child.

9. "If you look here," the biology teacher pointed to the diagram, "you can see the zygote, the very first stage of life after the sperm and egg merge."

10. Sage highlighted the textbook passage about the zygote, noting how this single cell embodies the potential for human development.

11. "The zygote forms right after fertilization," explained the doctor, helping the couple understand the early stages of pregnancy.

12. "Did you know this tiny zygote will turn into a baby?" the older sister asked gently as she prepared her younger sibling for the arrival of a new family member.

Practice Exercises

Instruction: Use this exercise to deepen your understanding of the lesson after reviewing each body part, such as the Adam's Apple or zygote, or after completing all the body parts in a particular letter set—A, B, or Z.

Task 1: Tagging Dialogues: Identify and list the dialogue tags used in the examples.

Task 2: Tracking Action Beats: Analyze the provided examples and identify action beats.

Task 3: Teasing Out Narrative Styles: Review the examples and distinguish between two narrative styles. Mark instances of deep POV that immerse you in a character's emotions or thoughts with a check mark (✓). Use an asterisk (*) to denote shallow POV instances, which focus primarily on surface-level actions or descriptions.

Task 4: Testing Your Skills with New Examples: Write four new phrases or short paragraphs incorporating an action beat and a dialogue tag. Use deep and shallow POV to explore different aspects of the body part discussed in this section.

Skill-Building Exercises

Sharpen your writing skills with these exercises centered on dialogue tags and action beats. Each task spotlights a different facet of character dialogue, such as identifying these components in popular literature, crafting dynamic conversations, or heightening emotion via action beats. Completing these activities equips you to compose engaging dialogues that truly animate your characters.

1. **Identifying Dialogue Tags and Action Beats**

   Read a selected passage from your favorite book. Identify and list all the dialogue tags and action beats used in the selection.

2. **Creating Dialogue with Tags and Beats**

   Write a short dialogue between two characters. Begin by only using dialogue, then go back and add dialogue tags and action beats to make the conversation more dynamic and engaging.

3. **Improving Dialogue with Tags and Beats**

   Take a piece of dialogue you've previously written. Try to minimize the use of common dialogue tags like "said" or "asked" and replace them with action beats that can convey the same information.

4. **Exploring Emotion through Action Beats**

   Choose an emotion (like happiness, anger, fear, etc.). Write a dialogue scene where a character experiences this emotion, using action beats to convey their feelings rather than explicitly stating them.

5. **Using Dialogue Tags for Characterization**

   Choose two characters with distinct personalities (for example, a shy person and an extrovert). Write a dialogue between them, using dialogue tags that reflect their speech patterns and personalities.

6. **Variety in Action Beats**

   Write a dialogue scene where the main character is doing something while talking (like cooking, driving, etc.). Use action beats to show what the character is doing and how it affects their conversation.

7. **Analyzing Published Works**

   Pick a favorite novel or short story. Analyze how the author uses dialogue tags and action beats to enhance the story. What can you learn from their style and technique?

Note: These exercises are designed to be practiced repeatedly. Mastery comes from continued application and practice.

Meet the Author

Franklyn James, originally from Jamaica and now a resident of Canada, is an educator, pastoral counselor, and artist with a rich background in theology and education. His life's work revolves around using his diverse knowledge and experience to foster holistic growth in others, a testament to his belief in the transformative power of personal experiences and acquired knowledge.

A passionate advocate for social justice and personal transformation, Franklyn's writing often reflects these themes. A critical thinker, he advocates for questioning traditional and contemporary rhetoric, bringing a unique and insightful perspective to discussions on inclusivity and justice. He is a prolific writer whose works include Tones of Transition, a narrative on communication; Shards of Longing, a book of dark poetry; and The Little Things We Take for Granted, a children's book intertwining poetry and coloring.

Franklyn's unique perspective and deep understanding are evident in his latest work, The Body in Narrative: A Writer's Guide to Character Reactions. This book reflects his commitment to utilizing his vast knowledge and experience to enhance storytelling, demonstrating the intricate connections between the human body and narrative.

Franklyn James is not just an author but a visionary whose multifaceted career is dedicated to educating, enlightening, and empowering others. As a clergy member and in writing, his work inspires and transforms those who encounter it.

www.ingramcontent.com/pod-product-compliance
Lightning Source LLC
Chambersburg PA
CBHW020441130626
46549CB00001B/253